Suzi
QUATRO
THROUGH MY WORDS

Published 2020

NEW HAVEN PUBLISHING LTD

www.newhavenpublishingltd.com

newhavenpublishing@gmail.com

Cover design © Pete Cunliffe

pcunliffe@blueyonder.co.uk

newhaven
publishing

ISBN: 978-1-912587-33-9

Contents

Me, cousin Jimmy, and best friend to this day, Linda, circa 1959

Suzi QUATRO

THROUGH MY WORDS

Prologue

Having written and published my coffee table size, illustrated poetry book, *THROUGH MY EYES*, my roaming mind moved ahead. Another thing on my bucket list was to do a lyric book.

I am a lyric/poetry/communicating/talking kind of person. I am wired that way. I can argue the toss into the wee hours of the morning with anyone about anything. So, when I go to write a song, I have much to dig into, my conversations with people from all walks of life, my unquenchable need to find out what makes people tick, even strangers, and my own ridiculously vulnerable artistic heart.

I had to go through a lot of songs, and have picked the ones I feel are important, although saying that, every song is important... they are your babies, and you give birth to them after much hard labour which is called 'life'. I kept it chronological because it made sense. You can see the development, beginning with me writing alone, then onto collaborations with my first husband, Len Tuckey, Chris Andrews ('Yesterday Man', amongst many), Rhiannon Wolfe, Shirlie Roden, Andy Scott, Steve Grant, Nat Allison, Laura Tuckey and Richard Tuckey. I have a funny quirk, and have lived by it my whole life. Yes, I talk poetically, yes I am very quotable, titles seem to fly out at will, the thing is... if I am with a writer/artist, guitarist etc... and one of these 'lines, titles' flies out... I always say to the person opposite me... okay... WE have to write this song together. It has always worked.

I want you to read, enjoy, and create your own reality... this is what true art is all about. What speaks to you speaks to you. As I am doing now...

This song was I guess my earliest solo composition, except for one I wrote for my mother, which got lost somewhere... all about this lonely woman sitting in a rocking chair, composed at the piano, damn, wish I could find that one!

'Brain Confusion' was written somewhere between 1969 and 1970, around a bass riff. It was first performed in Cradle (second wave of the Pleasure Seekers). This was at the time that my younger sister Nancy was added to the band as new lead singer. I took more of a back seat, having gone from singing 95% of the songs, playing bass and being the front person, to singing lead on maybe 6 songs per night... so quite a change. But the silver lining was... I became really really good on my instrument. And, for any sharp eared people, the original version went through quite a rewrite when I finally took it into the studio with Mickie Most producing.

Going through my songs and assembling this book, it seems 'lonely' is a common theme for me. Which is a little confusing... haha, brain confusion... because I was from such a huge family. In all honesty I always felt like the odd one out. This song reflects this. Also, it is one of the 2 songs I sang, along with 'Jailhouse Rock', on the night Mickie Most came to Detroit and saw Cradle live, and offered me a solo contract... and the rest, folks... is history.

• 2nd wave of all girl band, Cradle - note the bass player standing in the shadows, circa 1970.

BRAIN CONFUSION
(for all the lonely people)

(Suzi Quatro) Rak Pub.

V1
THERE'S TOO MANY PEOPLE
I CAN'T GET IT DOWN YEAH
RUNNING HIDING ROLLING SNEAKING
ALL OVER TOWN
I……… GOTTA GO YEAH
I SAID HEY, PEOPLE.. I SAID HEY… PEOPLE

V2 (modulate)
ALL DARKNESS, DARKNESS
SEEMS TO BE, SEEMS TO BE SO HOPELESS
AND I GOT THIS BRAIN, THIS BRAIN CONFUSION
WELL I'M TIRED I'M TIRED
I'M T- T -TIRED OF CHOOSING YEAH
I SAID HEY…. PEOPLE.. I SAID HEY… PEOPLE

CHORUS
(FOR ALL THE LONELY PEOPLE,
FOR ALL THE LONELY PEOPLE)

LIFE IS A FUNNY GAME, IT SEEMS SO STRANGE TO ME
WITH PEOPLE MASQUERADING AS THEY'LL NEVER BE
AND IF YOU LISTEN , AND DON'T KNOW WHAT I MEAN
LOOK INTO THE MIRROR, TELL ME WHAT YOU SEE
TELL ME ARE YOU A LITTLE LIKE ME
HEY LONELY PEOPLE. LONELY PEOPLE LIKE ME
LONELY PEOPLE, LONELY LONELY LONELY PEOPLE
GET READY EVERYBODY GET READY
(Repeat underneath)
LIFE IS A FUNNY GAME
IT SEEMS SO STRANGE TO ME
fade.

Released as the B-side to 'Rolling Stone' 1972,
featured on A's B's and Rarities, 2004

So, I made my decision to relocate to the United Kingdom.

I was 21 years old and the year was 1971. I was so damn excited, set my alarm at 5 a.m. regularly, down in my basement bedroom every single morning for the month before the big move.

Then, I went to get my coffee and doughnut on my bike, and after that, to Farm's Pier for a little sunshine... then home to write songs. I wrote and wrote and wrote and wrote, assembling around 30 tunes on a little cassette player. I was buzzing. I was high.

Finally got to London, Oct 31. My first recording company meeting was a couple of days later at Rak Publishing offices in Oxford Street, with Mickie. I played him my collection of songs... he fast forwarded non stop... oh boy, not good, and very uncomfortable. Finally he stopped... this song was not even finished yet... just a little snippet... but it had something.

Mickie said, 'Forget everything else... this is the one... work on THIS'... So I did. I guess he heard my 'style' in this.

The song is well before its time lyrically... and I honestly don't know where this came from...

I guess 'attitude' is in my DNA.

AIN'T YA SOMETHING HONEY

(Suzi Quatro) Rak Pub.

V1
I'M GETTING BOGGED DOWN
AND TIRED OF YOU PRETTY BOY
KEEPING YOUR BODY FED,
IS GETTING ME MIGHTY ANNOYED
ABOUT YOUR LOVE MAKING,
I AIN'T GETTING NO THRILLS
YOU SIT ALL DAY EXPECTING ME TO PAY YOUR BILLS.

CHORUS
AIN'T YA SOMETHING AIN'T YA SOMETHING HONEY
I GOTTA TAKE YOU IN HAND, I GOTTA MAKE YOU A MAN
I'M TIRED OF IT ALL, CAN'T YOU GUYS UNDERSTAND
WELL, AIN'T YA SOMETHING HONEY,
AIN'T YA SOMETHING HONEY
YOU'RE LOOKING PRETTIER THAN ME
WHAT THE HELL YOU TRYING TO BE

V2
YOU KNOW I'M FED UP, GET UP, COME ON
AND PUT ON YOUR PANTS
YOU USED ALL MY HAIRSPRAY LAST NIGHT,
GO OUT AND GET A NEW CAN
AND WHILE YOU'RE OUTSIDE,
PICK ME UP A BOTTLE OF WINE
HERE'S A FEW BUCKS I KNOW YOU AIN'T GOT A DIME
REPEAT CHORUS

V3
DO I HAVE TO KEEP ON TELLING YOU ALL OF THE TIME
CAN'T YOU SEE THIS SITUATION AIN'T WORKING SO FINE
ALL YOUR GOOD LOOKS,
YOU'RE NOTHING BUT A GREAT BIG BORE
ON YOUR WAY OUT BABY,
DON'T FORGET TO SHUT THE DOOR

REPEAT CHORUS

Released as B-side to 'Can the Can', 1973,
featured on The Girl From Detroit City box set 2014

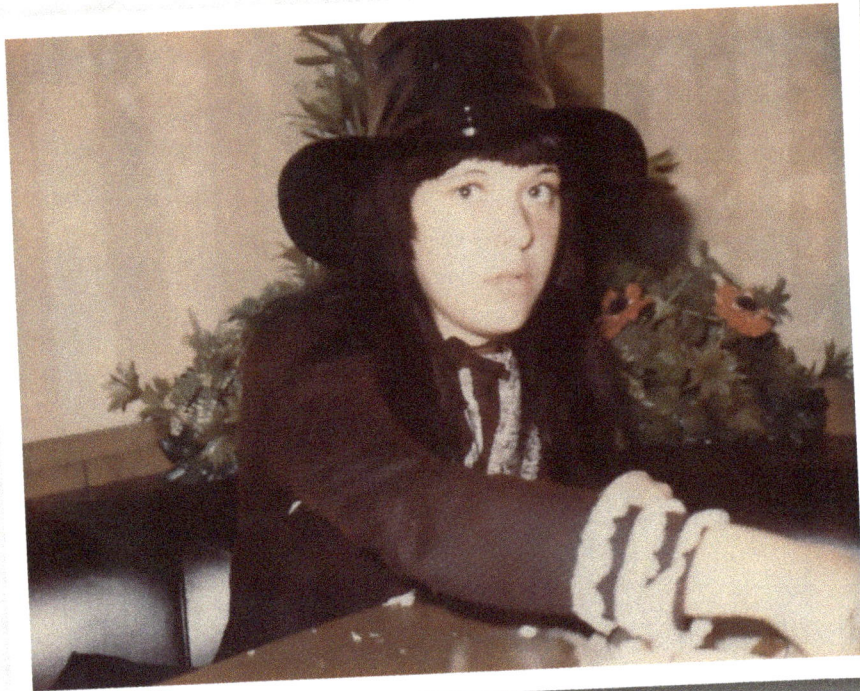

In London, Earls Court, tiny hotel room, all alone.

I was writing constantly trying to come up with that magical vehicle to stardom. We went into the studio recording the cream of the crop of my compositions with ace session musicians and yours truly on bass.

This next song is one of those we did. I always had a thing about 'blonde' women. Being a natural brunette, I laboured under the illusion that they did indeed 'have more fun'... well I have had dyed black hair, natural brown, highlighted and blonde for a while... and I can honestly say, this silly insecurity is no longer with me... I have FUN no matter what my hair colour is.

But that's now... this was 1972... young, innocent...ish... and definitely vulnerable (no -ish)... truly vulnerable... still am.

• Florida, dig the hat!, circa 1968

THE WICK THAT WAS

(Suzi Quatro) Rak Pub.

V1
I BEEN COMPETING WITH THE BLONDE NEXT DOOR
SHE NEVER GIVES ME NOTHING
BUT SHE'S ALWAYS GOT A BETTER SCORE THAN ME
I HAD TO GET SOME POINTS YEAH YEAH
IT MADE IT OBVIOUS THE OTHER DAY
WHEN I GAVE YOU A PRESENT
AND XMAS WAS GONE AND IT WASN'T YOUR BIRTHDAY
I HAD TO GET SOME POINTS YEAH YEAH
AND IT DON'T WORK ELECTRICALLY
BUT MAYBE YOU'LL THINK OF ME TONIGHT, YEAH YEAH
CHORUS
AND THEN YOU TOOK MY YELLOW CANDLESTICK
AND BURNED IT DOWN TO THE QUICK
NOW YOU GOT THE ONLY WICK THAT WAS
WHAT'S IT ALL ABOUT, WHY'D YOU PUT THAT FIRE OUT
NOW YOU GOT THE ONLY WICK THAT WAS
V2
MY TECHNIQUE IS AWKWARD I AIN'T GOT NO FINESSE
I ALWAYS SEEM TO OVERACT THE PART
WHEN I'M TRYING TO IMPRESS YOU
I KNOW I'M AWFULLY BLUNT… OH YEAH
I DON'T KNOW THE PROPER WAY TO GIVE YOU THE EYE
WHEN THEY HANDED OUT SOPHISTICATION
SOMEHOW IT PASSED ME BY
AND LEFT ME STANDING WITH MY NATURAL SELF, YEAH YEAH
BUT I COME TO YOU QUITE HONESTLY
AND OFFER YOU SIMPLY WHAT YOU SEE YEAH YEAH
REPEAT CHORUS
V3
I'M FIVE FEET TALL MY VOICE IS DEEPER THAN YOURS
I JUST CAN'T LOOK GRACEFUL, IN A CROWD I GET LOST
I'M TOO CLOSE TO THE FLOOR,
DON'T KNOW WHAT I BOTHERED FOR, YEAH YEAH
I GOT GOOD INTENTIONS SEEMS A SHAME TO ME
THAT YOU WON'T ACCEPT MY PRESENT
THE WAY THAT YOU FEEL IS ALMOST BROTHERLY
IF I WAS BLONDE, WOULD YOU LET ME HANG AROUND YEAH YEAH
DON'T ANSWER RIGHT AWAY, I CAN WAIT ANOTHER DAY, OKAY
REPEAT CHORUS.

Recorded in 1971/72, currently unreleased

So, here is the scenario. Tiny room, Aston House Villas... that's funny, villas!

Tiny bed, tiny wardrobe, tiny sink, tiny mirror, and no bathroom... the only thing that was huge was my loneliness... see... there's that word again.

I wrote songs with my bass, and a borrowed guitar, sitting on the bed, up until the wee hours of the morning... coffee, cigarettes, and creation... good combination.

Don't know where this came from but the idea was a dark skinned man, broke, needing to do something to make some money... so... he sells his curly hair... well, I was 21, I had a very active imagination, and I was on my own 99% of the time... so the ideas flew in and out at random. The recording of this is on my box set, The Girl From Detroit City. Impressive line up: Alan White from Yes, Rabbit on keys, the late but great Big Jim Sullivan on guitar, and yours truly... and I tell you what... we cooked.

CURLY HAIR FOR SALE

(Suzi Quatro) Rak Pub.

V1
BLACK MAN STANDING ON THE CORNER
GOTTA MAKE HIMSELF SOME BREAD
RAN HIS HAND ACROSS HIS AFRO
WENT HOME AND SHAVED HIS HEAD

CHORUS
THERE'S GOT TO BE ANOTHER WAY OF LIVING
IT AIN'T EASY
BEING BALD WHEN ITS FREEZING, HE SAYS,
CURLY HAIR FOR SALE

V2
THEY BOTH GOT MAD ABOUT THE WAY THINGS WERE
MADE A VERY COLOURFUL SCENE
WHY DO YOU HAVE TO SELL YOUR SOUL
JUST TO MAKE ENDS MEET

CHORUS
THERE'S GOT TO BE ANOTHER WAY,
OF LIVING IT AIN'T EASY
HOLDING HANDS AND SMILING, THEY SAY
CURLY HAIR FOR SALE

V3
MUST GROW, MUST GROW DOWN INTO THE NECK ZONE
JUST BEFORE THE COLLAR
CUT IT OFF AND STICK IT IN A BAG
STAND OUTSIDE AND HOLLAR

CHORUS
IT'S EASIER THIS WAY, LIVING TOGETHER
STANDING SIDE BY SIDE, THEY SAY
CURLY HAIR FOR SALE

Recorded in 71/72,
released on box set, Cherry Red Records,
The Girl From Detroit City 2014

This appeared on my first album. A very early Quatro/Tuckey composition. Great group of musos, Dave Neal on drums, Alistair McKenzie on keys, Len (ex husband) on guitar and yours truly. An excellent line up to be sure. Produced lots of great material.

I can honestly say, most of the first album was written on Chianti. Was quite cheap... and... you could stick a candle in the neck when you were finished and make a light out of it... we had a lot of lights!! This is all about my home town. I have never actually 'left' Detroit. It's in my heart and soul, and it is definitely in my bass lines, my backing vocal ideas, my dance moves... and my melodies.

What's that old saying... you can take the girl out of Detroit but you can't... (you know the rest).

• love this picture, circa 1974.

SHINE MY MACHINE

(Quatro/Tuckey) Rak Pub.

V1
DOWN IN MOTOR CITY I COME FROM
WHERE PEOPLE LIKE THEIR MUSIC LOUD
MOTOWN WAS BUILT ON THE EASTSIDE
DETROIT IS THE NAME OF MY TOWN

V2
FACTORY WORKERS, HIPPIES AND CREWCUTS
JUMPING UP AND DOWN IN THEIR SEATS
IN THE DAY TIME THEY SURE LOOK DIFFERENT
BUT AT NIGHTS IT'S JUST A ROCK N ROLL MEET

CHORUS
SO REV MY ENGINE, SHINE MY MACHINE
DRIVE ME, PET ME BABY
FILL ME WITH SLOW GIN

V3
SOUL BROTHER LIKES HIS OLD MOTOWN
THE GREASER STILL LOVES TO JIVE
YOU CAN'T KNOCK A ROCKER FOR ROCKIN'
IT'S WHAT KEEPS THIS CITY ALIVE

CHORUS
SO REV MY ENGINE, SHINE MY MACHINE
DRIVE ME, PET ME BABY
FILL ME WITH SLOW GIN.

Featured on Suzi Quatro, 1973

Some songs last an entire career. This one has been on stage since the day we recorded it and it still works. This is a true crazy story... here's the scene.

Doing a gig... somebody knocks on the dressing room door... it's a gender bender, full make up, tight dress, wig and heels... he sashays in... too interesting for us to leave him out in the hall don't you think!!... Anyway... we used to have this glycerine liquid for the boys to smear all over their bodies to look greasy and rock 'n' roll. Our lovely gender bender asked what it was... so Len said... 'Would you like some?'... and poured it into a beer... well... our gender bender drank it straight down without a second's pause... mmmmm... that's what you call getting an oil change from the inside!!

And this has now morphed live into including my famous bass and drum solo. Every time I try not to put the solo in the set... people go nutz.

THE GLYCERINE QUEEN

(Quatro/Tuckey) Rak Pub.

V1
BORN IN THE WORLD OF A FIFTY DOLLAR DREAM
TAILOR MADE CUT WITH A STRAIGHT BACK SEAM
JUST CAN'T RESIST THE TWILIGHT LIFE OF A QUEEN
TAKING POCKET MONEY GIVING SHADY SECRETS BACK
SOFT SPOKEN SILHOUETTE IS PART OF THE ACT
MOTHERS UNDERTAKER
COULDN'T DIG YOU A HOLE IN THE WALL

CHORUS
THE GLYCERINE QUEEN FIGHTING HARD TO WIN
(GLYCERINE QUEEN, GLYCERINE QUEEN)
WHATS A MATTER QUEENIE WON'T THEY LET YOU IN
(GLYCERINE QUEEN, GLYCERINE QUEEN)

V2
FIVE WILL GET YOU TEN YOU'RE ON THE PROWL AGAIN
PUT YOUR POT OF GOLD IN THE LION'S DEN
YOUR PARASITE MIND AIN'T THE TRULY RESPECTABLE KIND
YOUR LIFE STYLE PAST IS GONNA GET YOU SOON
SPEND A FEW YEARS IN A PADDED ROOM
A BOOK FULL OF BLUES
BAD MEMORIES TO PASS YOUR TIME

REPEAT CHORUS

WE ALL LAUGH AT THE GLYCERINE QUEEN
WE ALL LAUGH AT THE GLYCERINE QUEEN
WHAT'S THE MATTER QUEENIE
WON'T THEY LET YOU IN

REPEAT CHORUS

Featured on Suzi Quatro 1973

This got loads of airplay stateside, a weird tune, musically and certainly lyrically,

must blame the Chianti, again!! I remember working on this in our slightly improved hotel accommodations... we had moved from Earl's court to Cromwell Road... wow... things were indeed looking up... a bigger room... and... a bathroom. This was strange from the inception, chord structure strange, melody strange and even stranger, the lyrics. This song paints a picture. A vivid one.

• Classic Suzi shot, loved my EBO

SKIN TIGHT SKIN

(Quatro/Tuckey) Rak Pub.

V1
SKIN TIGHT SKIN, HAIR DYED AND WALKS LIKE RAINBOW
WHERE SHE BLOWS THE JOE KNOWS HER MIDDLE NAME
HIGH HEELS CLICK CLACK, HEY ARE YOU WALKING OR
STALKING

CHORUS
BECAUSE PEOPLE ARE TALKING DON'T YOU BELIEVE IT
DON'T YOU BELIEVE IT , DON'T YOU BELIEVE IT AH
PEOPLE ARE TALKING DON'T YOU BELIEVE IT
DON'T' YOU BELIEVE IT, AHHH

V2
MYSTIC INTERACTIVE MADE TO MEASURE WARM
CHIP SHOP MILK BAR PICK A NUMBER OFF THE WALL
HIGH TIME PLAY TIME, EVEN FIND TIME TO SLEEP SOME

CHORUS
BECAUSE PEOPLE ARE TALKING DON'T YOU BELIEVE IT
DON'T YOU BELIEVE IT, DON'T YOU BELIEVE IT AHH
PEOPLE ARE TALKING , DON'T YOU BELIEVE IT
DON'T YOU BELIEVE IT AH

Featured on Suzi Quatro 1973

Another one from the first album... you can hear it, the music was exciting, it was fresh, we were young, we were having hits, having fun, and definitely 'creating'... on a roll I believe is the phrase. Success breeds success. We were flying high.

This song was about a fictitious, for want of a better name, hooker... but... a hooker that had seen better days. I absolutely love the groove on this song... I adore my boogies.

Funny that this song never transferred to the stage... I wonder why... would have been a great stage number... maybe I will revive it.

ROCKING MOONBEAM

(Quatro/Tuckey) Rak Pub.

V1
HIP SHAKING BOOGIE BABY
YOU'RE NEVER GONNA BE NO QUEEN
PAST YOUR PRIME AND LOST YOUR TIME
NOW YOU'RE TWENTY YEARS PAST YOUR TEENS

V2
LIKE A BLAST FROM THE BLUNT LINE SPECIAL
AND THE DOCTORS ARE GROWING RICH
WHAT THE GUYS IN TOWN ARE BEING PASSED AROUND
AIN'T NO SEVEN YEAR ITCH

CHORUS
ROCKING MOONBEAM , YOU'RE A COOL OPERATOR
ROCKING MOONBEAM, YOU OLD HEARTBREAKER
ROCKING MOONBEAM, YOU TWO BIT TAKER
COVER UP YOUR FROWN
SO THE AGE WON'T SLOW YOU DOWN

(ROCKING MOONBEAM, ROCK ROCKING MOONBEAM)

REPEAT CHORUS

REPEAT FIRST VERSE

Featured on Suzi Quatro, 1973

Now, this song has a history. First of all, it was written true to life about how I felt within the family unit, and finally leaving my home for good.

The lyrics say exactly what I wanted to say about the situation. It is an emotional bluesy kind of tune, perfect for this kind of lyric. And, fast forward... when I do my first ever episode of Happy Days in 1977, it's the song I perform at Arnolds that gets me the gig.

This remains one of my favourites... and... one that should never be touched again... it is perfect as it is... as is the memory... as all memories should be... if it ain't broken don't fix it.

The title came from cat's eyes, those things in the road that light up... and the spelling... well... just blame the Chianti again... seemed like a good idea at the time... somebody light the candle!!

• Me and Henry (the fonz), Happy Days indeed

CATSIZE

(Quatro/Tuckey) Rak Pub.

V1
NOW I'M DONE, PLAYING THE FOOL
AND I PAID ALL MY CHILDHOOD DUES
I FIND THE MOUNTAIN MUCH STEEPER TO CLIMB
AM I JUST ONE, ONE OF THE CROWD

V2
I DECIDED, A FEW DAYS AGO
THERE'S NO ROOM, ROOM FOR ME IN THIS SHOW
I'VE CHANGED MY MAKEUP COMPLETELY THIS TIME
NOW I'M NOT ONE, ONE OF THE CROWD

CHORUS
SO GOODBYE, GOODBYE BLIND EYE
I'M GONNA FIND ME, A CAT'S EYE
OH GOODBYE, GOODBYE BLIND EYE
I KNOW WHAT I WANNA SEE

V3
NOW I'M DONE, PLAYING THE FOOL
AND I'VE PAID ALL MY CHILDHOOD DUES
I FIND THE MOUNTAIN MUCH STEEPER TO CLIMB
NOW I'M NOT ONE, ONE OF THE CROWD

REPEAT CHORUS

Featured on Suzi Quatro, 1973

We were in Los Angeles gigging and recording, very very busy, living in a rented house in the Hollywood hills. A very cool time in my life.

I was at a traffic light waiting for it to go green and happened to glance over at the Porsche next to me. I noticed a very arrogant looking man, and I mean very arrogant, you could feel his confidence coming off him in waves. I don't actually like these kind of men... anyway... I looked at him and thought... oh... there is an EGO IN THE NIGHT... and a song was born. Don't know what happened to the guy, don't know where the Porsche was going... and I don't care. I got a song out of it.

EGO IN THE NIGHT

(Quatro/Tuckey) Rak Pub.

V1
I SAW YOU WALKING DOWN THE STREET YOU WERE NEW
MY HEART IT NEARLY SKIPPED A BEAT, AND I KNEW
YOU WERE NOT THE LOVING KIND TO COOL
I KINDA PLAYED IT NOT SO NICE, TOO CRUEL
AH AH AH AH AH AH AH

CHORUS
HE WAS AN EGO IN THE NIGHT
A PERFECT PARTICLE IN FLIGHT
WHEREVER HE GOES HE'S SO RIGHT
HE WAS AN EGO IN THE NIGHT
AH AH AH AH AH .. IN THE NIGHT

V2
AND WHEN I LOOKED INTO YOUR EYES LIKE ICE
I WAS TRYING TO SOCIALISE BEING NICE
PROMISES OF PARADISE SAID YOU COULD
SUDDENLY I REALISED IT'S NO GOOD
MMMMMMMMM

REPEAT CHORUS

BRIDGE
AND THE WAY HE WEARS HIS HAIR
SURE TO MAKE THE WOMEN STARE
AND THE GAME HE PLAYS, HE KNOWS
AS A PASSING EGO GOES

REPEAT CHORUS

Featured on Rock Hard, 1980

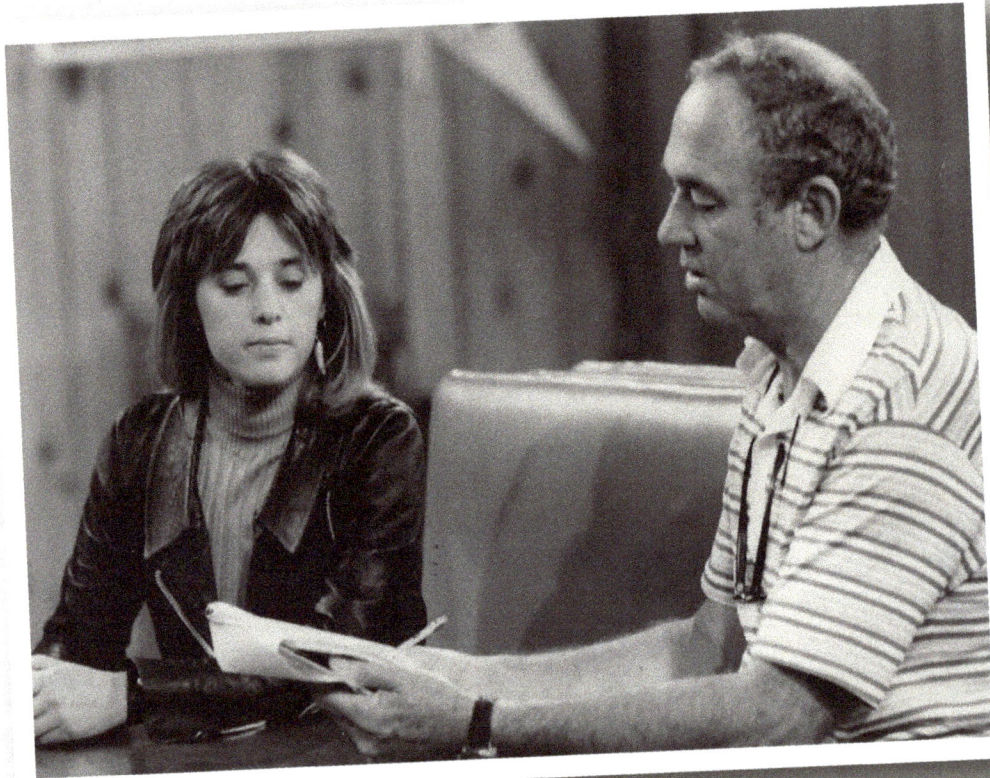

Wonderful song this one... Len gave me this chord structure... quite unusual... almost backwards. I played around with it... and came up with a title, which is often the first thing for me.

Hollywood... yep... Hollywood... so... what can this be about... I pondered and began to create the story. A small town girl, packs her bags and goes off to follow her dream. Will she make it... who knows... can she take it... who knows... Sound like somebody you know??

• In Hollywood Paramount studios, rehearsing script with director, Jerry Paris, just loved him.. r.i.p. circa 1977

HOLLYWOOD

(Quatro/Tuckey) Rak Pub.

V1
SHE PACKED HER BAGS ONE MOONLIT NIGHT
BOUGHT A TICKET ON A MYSTERY FLIGHT
TO A HEAVEN WHERE DREAMS DREAM
TO A HELL WHERE LOSERS WEEP
SHE'S GONE TO HOLLYWOOD
BRIGHT YELLOW LETTERS SHINE WAY UP HIGH
SWEET 16 SHE'S GOT STARS IN HER EYES
WILL SHE DRIVE IN CHAUFFEUR DRIVEN CARS
OR WILL SHE DIE OF A BROKEN HEART

CHORUS
SHE'S GONE TO HOLLYWOOD
OH HOLLYWOOD

V2
DOWN THE BOULEVARD OF DEVILS DELIGHT
SHE WALKS THE STREETS UNDER NEON LIGHTS
SO MUCH TO DO DON'T KNOW WHERE TO BEGIN
SO MUCH TO SEE IN THE CITY OF SIN

CHORUS
SHE'S GONE TO HOLLYWOOD, OH HOLLYWOOD
OH SHE FEELS SO GOOD
HI YA MAMA, HOW ARE YA DAD
BEEN THINKING BOUT YA PLEASE DON'T BE SAD
YOU'LL NEVER GUESS WHERE I'M CALLING FROM
I'LL BE A STAR BEFORE TOO LONG

CHORUS
CUZ I'M IN HOLLYWOOD, YES I'M IN HOLLYWOOD
OH IT FEELS SO GOOD, A STAR IN HOLLYWOOD

V5
LONG DISTANCE RINGING IN THE MIDDLE OF NIGHT
SAYING SOMETHING 'BOUT A SUICIDE
MISSING PERSON CALLING FROM THE COAST
YOUR DAUGHTER'S DEAD FROM AN OVERDOSE

CHORUS
HOLLYWOOD, SHE DIED IN HOLLYWOOD OH SHE FELT SO GOOD,
SHE DIES IN HOLLYWOOD, NOW SHE'S IN HEAVENWOOD,
OH SHE WAS FUCKING GOOD

Featured on Suzi…And Other Four Letter Words 1979

So... California dreaming for sure... spending lots of time there, recording Happy Days... gigging... writing... creating... existing... the thrust for this song was all the LA lost souls I used to see walking the streets... they were not of this world... and I invented a word for them... I called them Space Cadets. I was not a member of their family... you can blame my Catholic upbringing.

A real coooooool song. Production wise... Mike did the business on this... really did the business.

SPACE CADETS

(Quatro/Tuckey) Rak Pub.

V1
FLOAT DOWN THE AVENUE,
FLOAT ON 8 MILES HIGH
SPACE CADETS GONNA FLY ON DOWN THAT
RED RIBBONED SKY

CHORUS
SINGING OOOOO, SINGING OOOO WHERE DO WE BELONG
WHERE DID WE GO WRONG

V2
GOLDEN DREAMS IN SILVER SPOONS,
GIVE US ANYTHING OUR HEARTS DESIRE
PLASTIC SUNS I SEE PAPER MOONS
WELL I GUESS I MUST BE ON FIRE

CHORUS
SINGING OOO, SINGING OOO. WHERE DO WE BELONG
WHERE DID WE GO WRONG

V3
BRIGHT IS THE ANGEL LIGHT
GONNA SHINE SO CRYSTAL CLEAR
A VISION CAME SO SUDDENLY
THEN SOFTLY DISAPPEARED

CHORUS
SINGING OOOO SINGING OOO, WHERE DO WE BELONG
WHERE DID WE GO WRONG….. HIT IT

GOTTA FACE THOSE SPACE CADETS
FLOAT ON THOSE SPACE CADETS
GOTTA FACE THOSE SPACE CADETS
MMMM FLOAT ON THOSE SPACE CADETS.. YOU GOT TO

Featured on Suzi… And Other Four Letter Words 1979

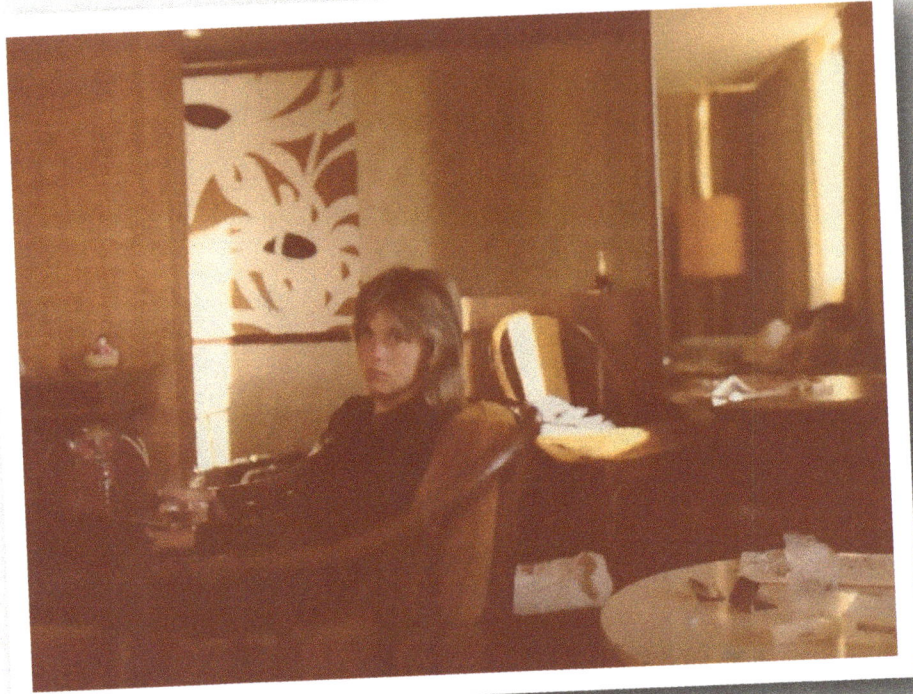

Now folks... this song is very very important. I talk a lot about 'lonely'... it's something I have known my entire life... I always feel 'lonely'... it's a constant, it is like a comfortable pair of jeans that I never want to throw away... because they still fit... I think if I ever lose this 'lonely'... I will not be the artist I am. Always wanted to write a song about my early days in London... before I knew anyone... before I fell in love, before I had a band, before I made any friends... this period between Oct 1971 and Oct 72... was probably the most alone I have ever been in my entire life. I revisited this feeling making the album Rock Hard... and as is my way, I made a positive out of a negative. I remember Mike waiting until the end of the evening after a long day of doing vocals, finally getting to this one... he wanted a particular sound. And he got it. It's a favourite amongst my fans. I did it live on the piano on my supposed (hahahaha) final Australian tour in 2015. I LIVED THIS SONG.

• Perth, Australia, outside concert rained off, '
  all dressed up nowhere to go'. circa 1974

LONELY IS THE HARDEST

(Quatro/Tuckey) Rak Pub.

V1
IN A RAINY CITY ALL ALONE
HAD NO PLACE I COULD CALL MY OWN
SMALL HOTEL ROOM SMOKING CIGARETTES
NOBODY KNOWS ALL THE PAIN I FELT

CHORUS
DO YOU BELIEVE WHEN I TELL YOU
THAT LONELY IS THE HARDEST
DO YOU BELIEVE WHEN I TELL YOU
THAT LONELY IS THE HARDEST… DAY OF ALL

V2
WRAP YOUR ARMS AROUND A SLEEPLESS NIGHT
COUNT THE HOURS TILL THE MORNING LIGHT
PIN UP PHOTOGRAPHS ON EMPTY WALLS
WRITING POEMS TO NO-ONE AT ALL

CHORUS
DO YOU BELIEVE WHEN I TELL YOU
THAT LONELY IS THE HARDEST
DO YOU BELIEVE WHEN I TELL YOU
THAT LONELY IS THE HARDEST…. DAY OF ALL

V3
LOOK OUT THE WINDOW, CROWDED STREETS BELOW
SEEMS EVERYBODY HAS SOMEPLACE TO GO
LOOK IN THE MIRROR TEAR STAINED EYES
CRY IN SILENCE FOR THE WASTED LIES

CHORUS
DO YOU BELIEVE WHEN I TELL YOU
THAT LONELY IS THE HARDEST
DO YOU BELIEVE WHEN I TELL YOU
THAT LONELY IS THE HARDEST.. DAY OF ALL

Featured on Rock Hard 1980

I get inspiration everywhere, conversations, people watching, t.v., magazines, newspapers, and of course what happens in my life. This idea came while reading the News of the World, when it was still in publication. There was an article about John Lennon; he was quoted, rightly or wrongly, as saying, 'I'm a prisoner on 72nd Street.' This struck a chord with me and out came the lyrics.

I remember strumming this chord sequence, badly, because I am not a guitar player, just good enough to write on. So tragic what happened to John, and even more strange that he got shot outside his apartment building, on 72nd Street!!

I became very good friends with his first wife Cynthia and stayed good friends until she passed away. I just loved her. As a birthday present she gave me four numbered portraits that she drew of John and I treasure them, as I treasured her.

This is one of the few songs I ever did on stage where I took off the bass, and just sang it. The others were 'The Race Is On', which I also just sang, centre stage, and on piano 'And So To Bed', 'Lonely Is The Hardest', 'Can I Be Your Girl', 'Sometimes Love Is Letting Go' and, years ago, 'Blind Emotions'.

SUICIDE

(Quatro/Tuckey) Rak Pub.

V1
GOODBYE AMERICAN DREAM
WITH YOUR LIFE INSURANCE AND PENSION SCHEMES WHOA OH
IT'S A LONELY RIDE DOWN GOLDEN HIGHWAYS
HOPE IS BLIND, YOU SHOOT FOR THE SKYWAYS
PROMISES TURNED TO DUST

CHORUS
AND IT'S SUICIDE
I'M A PRISONER IN 72ND STREET
AND IT'S SUICIDE
I'M A PRISONER IN 72ND STREET

V2
ASSEMBLY LINE, LIVING MACHINE
MASS PRODUCTION BOUGHT SIGHT UNSEEN WHOA OH
RULES AND REGULATIONS DAYS
PLEASE THE MAN OR LOSE YOUR PAY
AND YOU SELL YOUR SOUL TO SOCIETY

CHORUS
AND IT'S SUICIDE
I'M A PRISONER IN 72ND STREET
 AND IT'S SUICIDE
I'M A PRISONER IN 72ND STREET

V3
CRASH DOWN NO MORE LIES
DEEP DEPRESSION AFTER FEELING HIGH
WHEN PROMISES COME ALL UNDONE
ALL YOUR PROMISES TURN TO DUST

CHORUS
AND IT'S SUICIDE
I'M A PRISONER IN 72ND STREET
AND IT'S SUICIDE,
I'M A PRISONER IN 72ND STREET
I'M A PRISONER IN 72ND STREET
I'M A PRISONER IN 72ND STREET

Featured on If You Knew Suzi, 1978

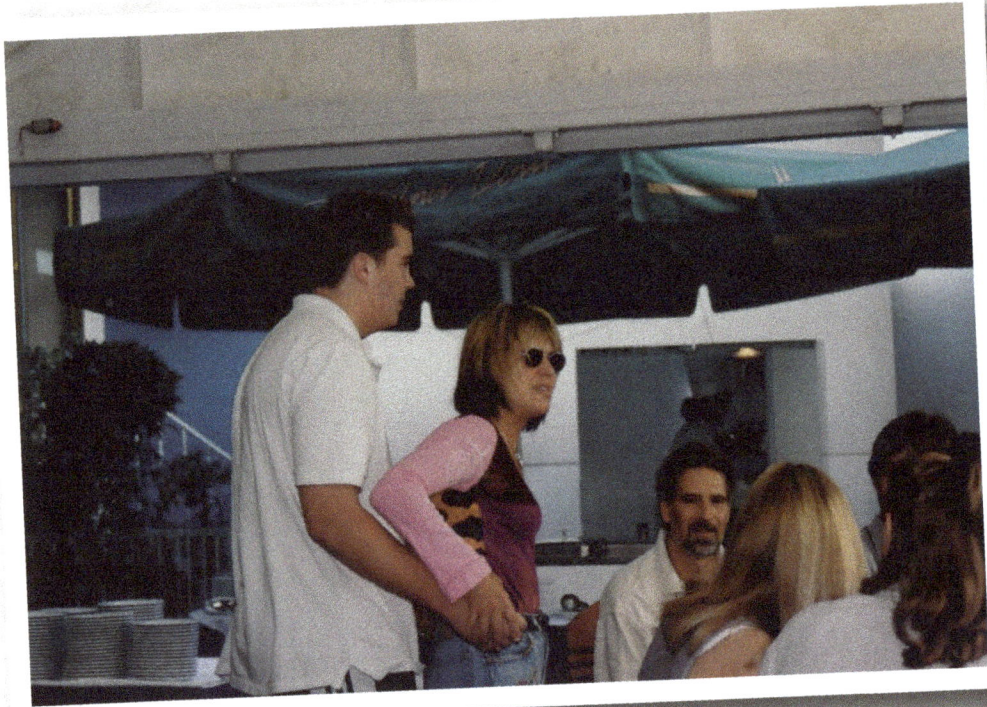

This idea came when gender bending was starting to become a real part of accepted society. I don't actually do labels, and I don't mind who or what people are, and I don't mind who does what with whom, and what your persuasions may be... I simply observe and write. This is about a guy who does not realise, or if he does, has not come out yet, and is still trying to make it with a woman.

I put myself in the position of 'knowing' him better than he knows himself for the purpose of this song.

I remember recording the track for this... and a couple of days later Mike coming into the studio and saying... sorry guys, we have to do the whole thing again. This could be a single, and it needs to be better. It did become a single. And we did do a better track. I know you're all wondering was this about somebody I knew... what do you think?

When my son was a little boy, he always thought this was written for him... awww.

He was too young to understand the lyric... he only caught 'mama's boy'... which he always was and always will be.

• 50th bday Berlin, 22,000 people, me and my little boy. circa 2000

MAMA'S BOY

(Quatro/Tuckey) Rak Pub.

V1
BY THE WAY HE LOOKS ACROSS HIS SHOULDER
AND THE WAY HE SEES ME THROUGH HIS EYE
IT'S IMPOSSIBLE TO DISGUISE, HE'S A MAMA'S BOY
SO CONFUSING TO MY SENSE OF HUMOUR
IS THE WAY HE HURTS SO EASILY
OH, ANYONE CAN SEE HE'S A MAMA'S BOY

CHORUS
FIRST HE HOLDS ME TOO SOFTLY
THEN HE TOUCHES ME, BARELY, MAMA'S BOY
THEN HE LOVES ME, TOO QUICKLY
OH HE'S EVERYTHING BUT MANLY, MAMA'S BOY, MAMA'S BOY

V2
IT'S A FUNNY KIND OF SITUATION
CAN'T RELATE TO WHAT IS HAPPENING
I'M TIRED OF MAKING TIME WITH A MAMA'S BOY
IT'S AN INSULT TO MY SENSE OF LIVING
WELL IT SEEMS I'M DOING ALL THE GIVING
I CAN'T WASTE ONE MORE NIGHT, HE'S A MAMA'S BOY

REPEAT CHORUS

V3
FIRST SHE TIES HIM TO HER APRON STRINGS
NOW HE NEEDS HER ADVICE ON EVERYTHING
OH, ANYONE CAN SEE, HE'S A MAMA'S BOY
DON'T KNOW WHY HE GETS INVOLVED WITH WOMEN
HE'S A CLOSET CASE WITH ALL THE TRIMMINGS
HE'S SUCH A PRETTY THING, HE'S A MAMA'S BOY
NANANANANANNA…. NANANANANANA

MAMA'S BOY *REPEAT AND FADE*

Featured on Suzi… And Other Four Letter Words, 1979

Dreamland Records died and I was cut adrift. We made a deal with Polydor. I wrote some songs on this album with Chris Andrews ('Yesterday Man'... amongst many many others, good writer and singer still working today, and still a friend), and we recorded the whole thing at his home studio.

I fell pregnant with my firstborn during the recording of this album, after having suffered a miscarriage 6 months previously. I was over the moon to finally be pregnant again. It was an interesting exercise to do songs this way. Previously I had only written alone or with Len. This opened me up to a new experience. It was a good album called Main Attraction... and on the cover... I am sitting in a car... hiding my big belly!!

Doing this lyric book, I am wondering if I should write to the people who publish the dictionary of English words... and request that after the word 'lonely' it should say, Suzi Quatro... just a thought.

THE MAIN ATTRACTION

(lyrics S. Quatro, Rak Pub, music C. Andrews, Carnaby Music Ltd.)

V1
DREAMS ARE HARD TO FIND,
I'VE BEEN SEARCHING ALL MY LIFE
ALL THOSE COLD AND LONELY NIGHTS YOU WERE ON MY MIND
SEEMS A HUNDRED YEARS AGO,
WHEN I WALKED OUT THAT DOOR
I WAS BLIND I COULD NOT SEE,
HOW MUCH YOU MEANT TO ME

CHORUS
HERE WE STAND IN THE MORNING LIGHT
HONEY DON'T YOU KNOW YOU'RE THE MAIN ATTRACTION
HAND IN HAND IN THE QUIET OF NIGHT
HONEY DON'T YOU KNOW, YOU'RE THE LIGHT OF LOVE
BABY TONIGHT

V2
I SOFTLY SAID GOODBYE,
TO THE SADNESS IN YOUR EYES
AND THE PAIN IT PUT ME THROUGH
BROUGHT ME BACK TO YOU

REPEAT CHORUS

BRIDGE
I WASTED PRECIOUS TIME, I LEFT MY HEART BEHIND
I FOUND MYSELF ALL ALONE
I HAD TO TRIP AND FALL, I HAD TO LOSE IT ALL
TO FIND MY WAY BACK HOME

REPEAT CHORUS

Featured on Main Attraction, 1982

I remember during the writing/recording of this album, Chris's then wife Gloria said,

Come on... write something in the same vein as 'If You Can't Give Me Love', that's one of Suzi's best ones. And this is in a similar vein. I enjoyed writing this one.

Simon Bates, who was on Radio 1 at the time, played this on his show and said, Here's a song that Mickie Most will be glad to hear. Well Mickie may have been glad, but I was gladder... (is that a word?) Artistic licence. And now to the song.

• Nice bass, still have it, circa, who knows?

HEART MADE OF STONE

(lyrics S. Quatro, Rak Pub/music C. Andrews/Carnaby Music Ltd.)

V1
WELL I GAMBLED PLAYED THE GAME
TOOK MY CHANCES ONCE AGAIN
GUESS I'M ALWAYS A FOOL FOR LOVE
WHEN I'M FEELING LONELY
AND I KNOW HE'LL CAUSE ME PAIN
BUT I NEED HIM JUST THE SAME
CUZ I AIN'T GOT THE STRENGTH TO SAY NO,
WHEN THE NIGHTS ARE LONELY

CHORUS
ANOTHER HEART MADE OF STONE, AND A LOVE I CANNOT OWN
AND IT CUTS ME TO THE BONE, ANOTHER HEART OF STONE
NO MATTER WHAT I DO OR SAY, IF I GIVE IT ALL AWAY
IT STILL WON'T MAKE ME STAY, ANOTHER HEART OF STONE

V2
YOU KNOW FOOLS THEY LOVE AND RUN
AND I KNOW I'VE BEEN FOOLED BY SOME
ALL THOSE PROMISES MADE
DISAPPEAR IN THE HAZE OF THE MORNING SUN
I WANNA TAKE YOU IN MY ARMS
WANNA DRINK IN ALL YOUR CHARMS
EVEN THOUGH IT'LL TEAR ME APART WHEN THE NIGHT IS OVER

REPEAT CHORUS

V3
THEY SAY LOVING RULES THE NIGHT
BUT YOU KNOW THAT LOVE AIN'T RIGHT
IF IT'S GIVEN TO ONE WHOSE AFFECTION HAS NO MEANING
AND SO I GAMBLE LIKE BEFORE
THEN I'LL TAKE JUST A LITTLE BIT MORE
CUZ YOUR ARMS HOLD A THOUSAND REASONS
TO KEEP ME DREAMING

REPEAT CHORUS

Featured on Main Attraction 1982

This one I had the title first, unusual because it was kind of 'out there'... I was doing a song that had no actual logic.

If I was an actual 'stoner' I would have written stuff like this more often... I was not. But hey, if we're talking fantasies...
I don't believe in mono... I want mine in stereo.

FANTASY IN STEREO

(S. Quatro), Rak Pub.

V1
I WAS GETTING INTO DOUBLE VISION
I WAS NEARLY BLINDED BY EMOTION
TOOK ME BY SURPRISE I LOST CONTROL
SUDDENLY I FELT MY SENSES GOING
FADE AWAY, PICTURE YOU, PICTURE ME
ENDLESSLY

CHORUS
FANTASY IN STEREO, FANTASY IN STEREO, FANTASY IN STEREO
TURNING ME OVER

V2
I WAS GETTING HOOKED, SO SENTIMENTAL
I WAS RIDING HIGH, ON INNUENDO
YOU WERE MAKING EYES, AND TAKING CHANCES
WE WERE MAKING WAVES, AND NEW ROMANCES
SUDDENLY, FADE AWAY, YOU AND ME
ENDLESSLY

REPEAT CHORUS

V3
I WAS OUT REACHING OUT FOR SOMETHING BETTER
WE WERE REACHING OUT TO TOUCH EACH OTHER
STANDING CLOSE TO ME , I FELT YOU TREMBLE
WAS IT IN A DREAM, I LET MY HEART GO

REPEAT CHORUS

Featured on Main Attraction 1982

Chris, during the recording of this album, had found a girl singer from Germany. He was doing some songs with her in the studio. She was very unusual looking, and definitely had the X factor. We wrote this song with her in mind. Chris did the music and I did the lyrics. She stayed at the house for a few nights. I am using the word 'strange' here... I am very perceptive, but she was hard to read. Nobody got in and nobody got out, hence the title... I wonder what her star sign was? And I wonder where she is now?

• Cradle band days, Halloween gig, boo!!!

CHAMELEON

(Lyrics S. Quatro, Rak Pub/music C. Andrews, Carnaby Music Ltd.)

V1
FLASH, HERE I AM, YES IT'S HARD TO UNDERSTAND
LIKE THE GREY OF NIGHT MY EYES ARE DECEIVING YOU
SO DON'T BE AFRAID, OF MY FELINE KIND OF GRACE
I WILL MELT YOU LIKE ICE, IN THE COOLEST OF NIGHTS

CHORUS
EVERY CHANGING FACE OF A CHAMELEON
DEVIL OR ANGEL IN DISGUISE
NEVER KNOW WHICH ONE YOU CAN BELIEVE IN
WITH THE EVER CHANGING FACE OF A CHAMELEON

V2
THIEVES STEAL AWAY, AND THE FOOL BEGINS TO PLAY
AS THE MUSIC OF MY SMILE HYPNOTISES YOU
YOU BURN LIKE A FIRE, WITH THE FLAMES OF YOUR DESIRE
I'M A STRANGER OF LOVE, I'M THE SOFTEST TO TOUCH

REPEAT CHORUS

BRIDGE
I'LL ALWAYS BE, A PARODY OF MAKE BELIEVE
I CAN MASQUERADE MY FEAR, CRY A SINGLE TEAR
SO SEE WHAT I AM, AND DON'T TRY TO UNDERSTAND
I'M A MYSTERY OF LIFE, I'M THE BLACKNESS IN WHITE

REPEAT CHORUS

Featured on Main Attraction 1982

So after trying for 2 years, finding out I had low fertility, going on fertility treatment, getting pregnant then miscarrying at 3 months... I finally had a baby. Not easily either. 16 hours, no good, then emergency and put out cold for a C-section, but it didn't matter... I HAD MY BABY ATLAST.

Of course this inspired a song. This was recorded about a year after the birth, but was not released until the nineties, on Unreleased Emotion. We did it at Rak Studios.

• a baby at last, 1982, look at that hair

EVERYTHING I EVER WANTED

(Quatro/Tuckey) Rak Pub.

V1
LONELY DAYS LONELY NIGHTS
THEN I SAW THAT LOOK IN YOUR EYES
OH YOU DO SOMETHING SPECIAL TO ME
FOUND THE WAY, TO MY HEART
MADE ME FEEL WHAT LOVE'S ALL ABOUT
OH YOU DO SOMETHING SPECIAL TO ME

CHORUS
CUZ YOU'RE EVERYTHING I EVER WANTED ,
YOU'RE EVERYTHING I EVER NEEDED.

V2
I WAS COLD, RUNNING WILD,
TILL YOU MELTED ME WITH YOUR SMILE
YOU PUT THE SUNSHINE INTO MY LIFE
FEELING LOST IN A CROWD
NOW I'M PROUD TO SAY IT OUT LOUD
YOU PUT THE SUNSHINE INTO MY LIFE

CHORUS
YOU'RE EVERYTHING I EVER WANTED
YOU'RE EVERYTHING I EVER NEEDED
YES AND ALL THE THINGS I HAVE BEEN DREAMING OF
YOU'RE EVERYTHING I EVER WANTED

Recorded in 1983, released on Unreleased Emotion 1998

I have a distinct memory of Len coming up and saying... You should write a song called 'Can I Be Your Girl'... so I did. I wrote this originally on guitar, and it was recorded around the same time as the previous song... and again... not released until the Unreleased Emotions album. Eventually I put this song on the stage. I had the idea to do it at the piano... worked out chords and what would be sympathetic to me singing and playing the piano on stage... then... my son and my second husband Rainer (married 27 years at the time of writing this book) came into where I was practising and I said... See how you like this version... of course I still have to add instruments. I played and sang it. They both said at the same time... Why add anything, that's perfect. So it became my solo moment in the show at the piano. Who knew?

I dedicate this live on stage, every show I do, to my dad for giving me my career, and my mother for giving me my life.

• Can I be 'your' girl?

CAN I BE YOUR GIRL

(Quatro/Tuckey) Rak Pub.

V1
WELL I'M TELLING YOU NOW THINGS I PROMISED I'D NEVER SAY
AND I'M TAKING MY CHANCES I WON'T FALL,
FLAT ON MY FACE
YES THERE'S NO DENYING I NEED YOU SO
IT'S TOO LATE NOW TO EVER LET YOU GO

CHORUS
CAN I BE YOUR GIRL,
I DON'T WANNA WASTE MY TIME
CAN I SHARE YOUR WORLD
I DON'T WANNA WAIT IN LINE
CAN I BE YOUR GIRL

V2
WELL I SAID YOU'VE BE FREE YES I TOLD YOU,
NO STRINGS ATTACHED
BUT HOW COULD I HAVE KNOWN THAT WE'D END UP,
THE PERFECT MATCH
AND I'D FIND MYSELF SO IN LOVE WITH YOU
IT'S TOO LATE NOW TO SAY GOODBYE TO YOU.

REPEAT CHORUS

Recorded in 1983, released on Unreleased Emotion 1998

One of my favourite lyrics of all time.
This happened to me. It is a very honest song.

It could have gone in my poetry book, Through My Eyes,
but I am glad I saved it... because it is a lyric... and it is a
beautiful song. When I wrote my musical with Shirlie
Roden, book by Willie Rushton called Tallulah Who? (and
played Tallulah Bankhead, wow, dream come true for me)...
we added this number even though it had nothing at all to do
with the story. We found a scene it worked perfectly in. This
never made it live to my rock stage though... don't know why.
Maybe it is too theatrical.

• *Me sleeping in my bed, this child is still alive*

TOUCH THE CHILD IN ME

(S.Quatro) Butterfly/Rak Pub.

V1
WHEN MORAL CODES AND HYPOCRISY
ARE STANDING SIDE BY SIDE
CAN YOU KEEP THE CHILD ALIVE
WHEN FLAMES SUBSIDE, THE EMBERS DIE,
LOVE'S BATTLEFIELD OF BONES
THE CHILD IN ME DID NOT SURVIVE, WOMAN STANDS ALONE

V2
ARMS AROUND A DREAM
I NEEDED TO BELIEVE IN LOVE
AND THE HEROES OF THE NIGHT
TIMES GREW HARD, WE DRIFTED APART
SHATTERED ILLUSIONS OF LIFE
THE CHILD IN ME DID NOT SURVIVE, WOMAN STANDS ALONE

CHORUS
SHE WALKS THAT ROAD ALONE, LIKE A HEART WITHOUT A HOME
OH, HEROES OF THE NIGHT, TOUCH THE CHILD IN ME

V3
A FEELING DEEP INSIDE EXPLODES
A FEVER SHE COULD NOT DENY
BROUGHT A STRANGER TO HER DOOR
LUST IN HIS HEART HE RIPPED ME APART
AND GOT ME BEGGING FOR MORE
THE CHILD IN ME DID NOT SURVIVE, WOMAN STANDS ALONE

BRIDGE
THIS WORLD IS LONELY, SO LONELY,
AND YOU FEEL LIKE YOU CAN'T GO ON
SOMEBODY HOLD ME, REACH OUT YOUR ARMS, RELEASE ME

CHORUS
SHE WALKS THAT ROAD ALONE, LIKE A HEART WITHOUT A HOME
OH HEROES OF THE NIGHT TOUCH THE CHILD IN ME
(CAN ANYONE REACH OUT AND TOUCH HER)
TOUCH THE CHILD IN ME
(SOMEBODY TO STAY HERE AND LOVE HER)
TOUCH THE CHILD IN ME

Featured on In the Spotlight deluxe version, In the Dark, 2012, Cherry Red Records

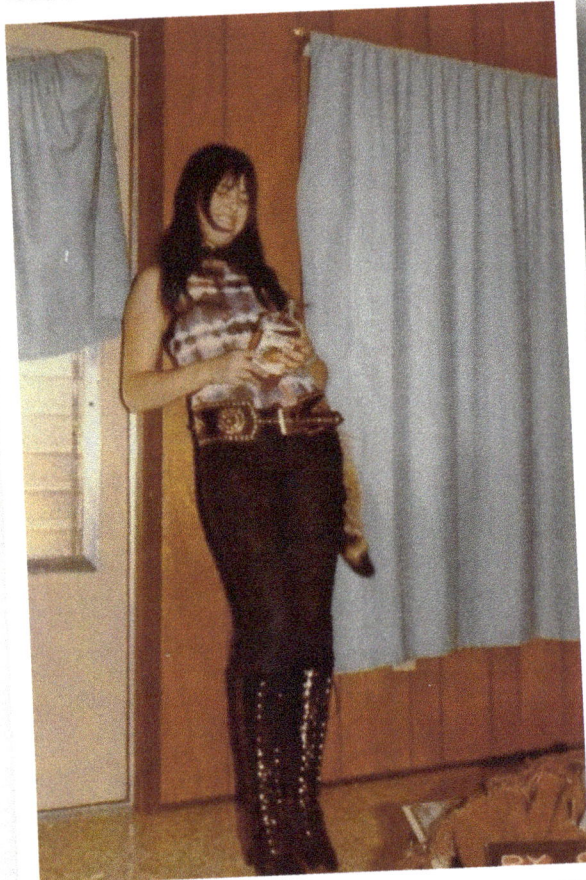

Interesting little tune and interesting lyrics on this one... very unlike Suzi... don't know where this came from style wise... Billie Holiday, Ella Fitzgerald, Lena Horne, even Peggy Lee, any of those classic singers could have done this justice. Could have been done in a bar in New Orleans, on a river boat, could have been in the t.v. series Roots... get the picture. This never made it onto a recording... it only exists as a demo. I had a very creative time late 80s early 90s while my marriage was falling apart. Creation always saves me. Like I said... if I ever lose the lonely... I die... simple as that. Three key words that describe me... communicator, creative and entertaining... okay... maybe there are more!!

• strange picture, didn't even drink back then, oh well! circa 1970

3 X LOSER

(Quatro/Tuckey) Rak Pub.

V1
I GAVE YOU MY LOVING, THE BEST THAT I HAD
SO WHY DID YOU HURT ME, I'M FEELING SO BAD
IT'S SO DAMN CONFUSING, TO WANT YOU THE WAY YOU ARE
BUT I'M A 3 X LOSER, WITH A ONE MAN HEART

V2
THERE'S NO CRITICISING I BREAK WHEN I LOSE
TOO MANY EXCUSES, I LOOK SUCH A FOOL
WHEN ALL I DESIRE IS TEARING MY WORLD APART

CHORUS
BUT I'M A 3 X LOSER, WITH A ONE MAN HEART
JUST A MIDNIGHT BLUESER, WITH EMPTY ARMS,

BRIDGE
I'M DYING, I CAN'T STOP CRYING
THE WHOLE SITUATION IS MYSTIFYING
SO MUCH LYING, CHEATIN' AND DENYING
DON'T YOU UNDERSTAND MY LIFE IS IN YOUR HANDS
I'M A 3 X LOSER, TRYING TO KEEP MY MAN

V3
I'VE NEVER BEEN HARD NO, I CAN'T PLAY IT COOL
I WAIT BY THE PHONE, IT'S THE BEST I CAN DO
BUT I AIN'T COMPLAINING I LOVE YOU THE WAY YOU ARE

CHORUS
BUT I'M A 3 X LOSER, WITH A ONE MAN HEART
JUST A MIDNIGHT BLUESER WITH EMPTY ARMS

REPEAT BRIDGE

V4
I GAVE YOU MY LOVING, THE BEST THAT I HAD
SO WHY AM I LONELY, AND FEELING SO SAD
THERE'S NO EXPLANATION, I LOVE YOU THE WAY YOU ARE

CHORUS
AND I'M A 3 X LOSER, WITH A ONE MAN HEART
JUST A MIDNIGHT BLUESER, WITH EMPTY ARMS
ONE MORE LONELY WOMAN, TRYING TO KEEP HER MAN
I'M A 3 TIME LOSER.... DOING THE BEST I CAN.

Featured on In the Spotlight deluxe, In the Dark, 2012

All photographs on this page: **Chell Carr**

All photographs on this page: **David Alcott**

All photographs on this page: **Pat Doonan**

All photographs on this page: **Lynn Chapman**

All photographs on this page: **Linda Buchanan**

All photographs on this page: *Julie Ainsworth*

Another one recorded late 80s and not released until 90s on Unreleased Emotion. Every now and again I come up with one of these, for want of a better word, sweet, kind of cute songs, just bordering on pop... but not quite. I was nearing the end of my marriage and I guess every song took on a surreal aspect. I created, I imagined, I fantasised a different life, every song, every lyric, poems, every poem, writing the musical, whatever... it was all an escape... and needing to escape inside, creativity is definitely therapeutic.

I still do it to this day.

SECRET HIDEAWAY

(Quatro/Tuckey) Rak Pub.

V1
NIGHT HAS A THOUSAND EYES, HIDING IN PARADISE
WAITING FOR TRUE LOVE WAYS, OPENING HEAVEN'S GATE
IF YOU WILL TAKE A CHANCE, YOU JUST MIGHT FIND ROMANCE
I'M ASKING YOU TO BE, THE MEANING OF LIFE TO ME

CHORUS
SO DO YOU WANT TO COME TO MY
 SECRET LITTLE HIDEAWAY
DO YOU WANT TO SHARE
THE MYSTERIES OF MY SOUL
I CAN FLY YOU TO THE PLACES
YOU'VE BEEN DREAMING OF
MY SECRET HIDEAWAY,
HIDE AWAY, MY LOVE

V2
MOVING SO SENSUAL, KISSING WHEN LIGHTS ARE LOW
WALKING ALONG THE SAND, WHISPERING HAND IN HAND
ALL THIS I PROMISE YOU, I DON'T MEAN TO FRIGHTEN YOU
I'LL GIVE YOU EVERYTHING IF YOU'LL FALL IN LOVE WITH ME

CHORUS
SO DO YOU WANT TO COME TO MY
SECRET LITTLE HIDEAWAY
DO YOU WANT TO SHARE
THE MYSTERIES OF MY SOUL
I CAN FLY YOU TO THE PLACES
YOU'VE BEEN DREAMING OF
MY SECRET HIDEAWAY
HIDE AWAY, MY LOVE

Recorded in 1983, on Unreleased Emotion in 1998

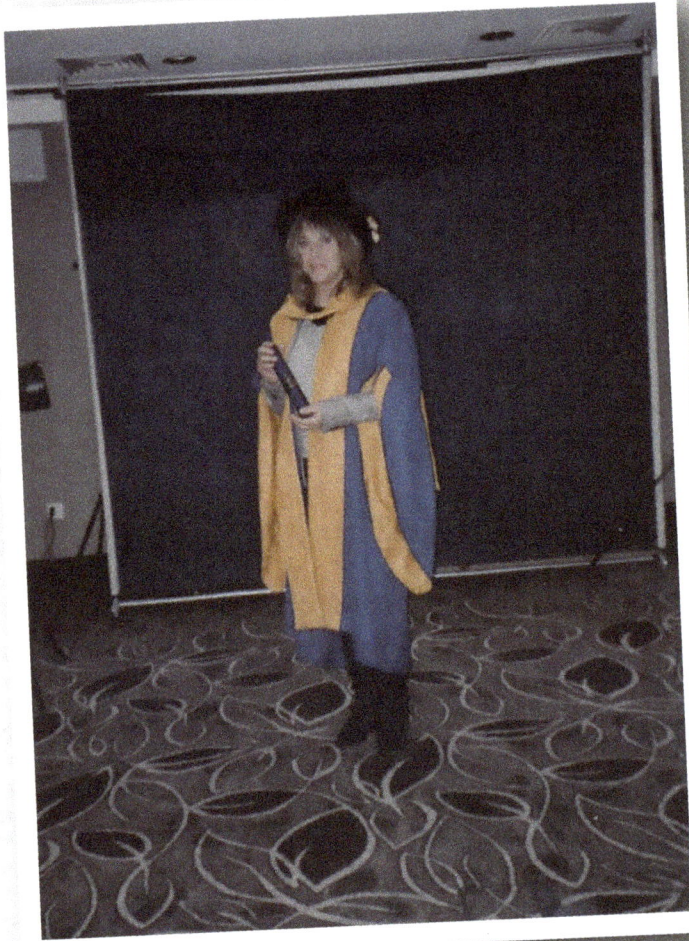

I was on a roll at this time... writing lots of stuff... poetry and songs... all about love that didn't quite work out the way I wanted it to. I love loving, I love being in love, I love the promise of love... yep... a hopeless romantic. Read between the lines. My story is all here... through my words.

• Didn't graduate high school, becoming honorary doctor of music, Cambridge University, circa 2016, 'pardon me!!!'

PARDON ME

(Quatro/Tuckey) Rak Pub.

V1
LOVE AND DEVOTION,
WELL YOU SAID YOU'D NEVER LEAVE ME
THIS SITUATION IS GETTING OUT OF HAND
CUZ YOUR AFFECTION
I KNOW YOU'RE GIVING SOMEONE ELSE AND
I SHOULD HAVE KNOWN THAT
YOU'RE THAT KIND OF MAN
AND DARLING LISTEN TO ME, I DON'T WANT TO PLAY
HONEY I'VE GOT SOMETHING TO SAY

CHORUS
AND IT'S PARDON ME, YOU BETTER TURN AROUND AND RUN
YES IT'S PARDON ME, I GUESS IT MEANS I'VE HAD ENOUGH
WELL IT'S ONE, TWO, THREE TIMES BABY,
LOOK AT WHAT YOU'VE DONE
I SAID PARDON ME , YOU KNOW
I'VE FINALLY HAD ENOUGH, OF YOUR LOVE

V2
YES I WAS HUNGRY,
YOU PROMISED ME MOST EVERYTHING AND
MY NIGHTS WERE LONELY
WHEN I LET YOU IN
A LITTLE ROMANCE
GOES A LONG LONG WAY AND
IT TAUGHT ME A LESSON
ALMOST DID ME IN
AND DARLING LISTEN TO ME I DON'T WANT TO PLAY
HONEY, I GOT SOMETHING I GOT TO SAY

REPEAT CHORUS

BRIDGE
OH DARLING YOU WERE ALWAYS SPECIAL TO ME
AND HONEY, NOW YOU'RE SIMPLY NOTHING TO ME
(NOTHING TO ME)

REPEAT CHORUS

Recorded 1983, released on Unreleased Emotion 1998

On this batch of songs, I seemed to have moved away from writing about 'me', except for 'Everything I Ever Wanted'... and started to write as an observer. I think what was happening was... I had had my first baby... and there was a definite adjustment to be made by both Mom and Dad. I could not be so intense with my thoughts, I had another person to think about. So, the songs came out more as 'songs'... using my knowledge as a musician and lyricist, and just creating... not pulling it out of my guts... which was the normal way... and something I returned to with a vengeance in 1991 and have stayed there ever since.

Enjoy the exercise. Nothing is ever wasted... each baby you give birth to (song wise and person wise) teaches you something. And actually, reading these lyrics all these years later... it is very possible, very very possible, I had a certain person in mind from long ago.

STARRY NIGHTS

(Quatro/Tuckey) Rak Pub.

V1
OH SO YOUNG, SPECIAL ANGEL, ALWAYS MAGICAL TO ME
YOU WERE SUCH AN ORDINARY GUY
HOW YOU LED ME TO YOUR HEAVEN
THEN YOU WHISPERED TENDERLY
HOW CAN SOMETHING WRONG, FEEL SO WONDERFUL
BUT WHAT COULD I DO, I WAS SO IN LOVE WITH YOU

CHORUS
STARRY NIGHTS, I REMEMBER
WHEN OUR HEARTS WE SURRENDERED
HOW THE SWEETNESS OF YOUR TOUCH LINGERED ON
FROM A CHILD TO A WOMAN, FROM THE DARKNESS
CAME THE MORNING
LOST FOREVER, STARRY NIGHTS I REMEMBER

V2
WHEN I MET YOU I WAS TAKEN SO COMPLETELY BY SURPRISE
WRAPPED IN YOUR ARMS SO SOFT AND WARM
FOR THE FIRST TIME I WAS SHAKEN, BY THE PROMISE IN YOUR EYES
KISSES SWEETER THAN WINE, YOU SMILED SO BEAUTIFUL
BUT WHAT COULD I DO, I WAS SO IN LOVE WITH YOU

REPEAT CHORUS

BRIDGE
ALL THOSE DREAMS THAT WE LIVED ON,
IN THAT FORGOTTEN TIME
FOR ONE MINUTE OF YOUR LOVING, I WOULD DIE DIE DIE

REPEAT CHORUS

Recorded 1983, released on Unreleased Emotion, 1998

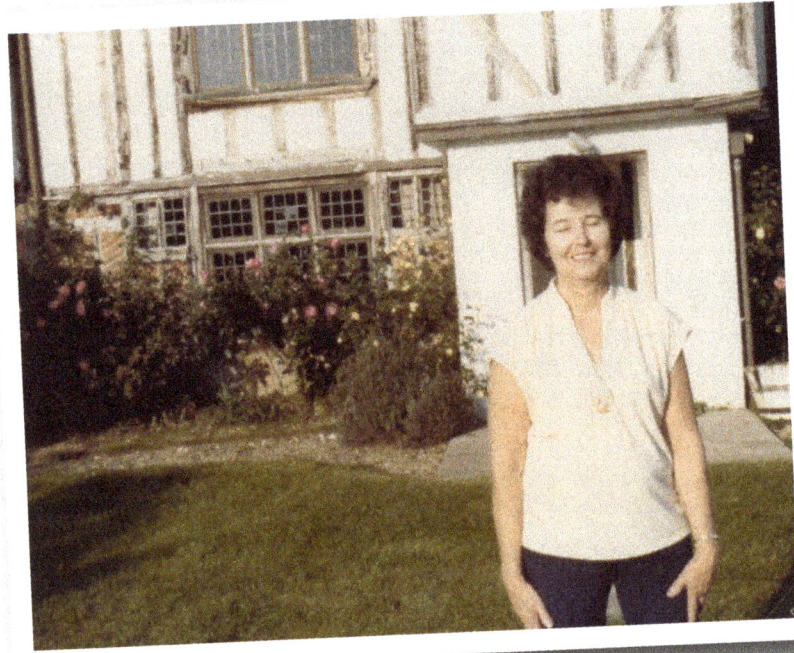

The mind works in funny ways, criss crossing situations, memories and triggers. Typing out the last song triggered my memory which triggered the need to include this song. This is about the married man I fell in love with, age 18; it's all in Unzipped, my autobiography, and in Through My Eyes, my poetry book, and now in this. Seems this guy left quite an impression in my heart and soul. Your first grown up love sinks deep inside, and never leaves you... Although I have mellowed a little in my attitude, because years put things in the right place. Wiser than you is how I felt about things for a long long time. And, if I am honest... most likely still do.

• my mother, could never fool her, she was my strength, and always, 'wiser than me'! circa 1980

WISER THAN YOU

(S. Quatro/Tuckey) Rak Pub.

V1
YOU MESSED MY MIND, DESTROYED MY SOUL
HOW WAS I SUPPOSED TO KNOW ABOUT THE POWER OF LOVE
YOU WERE WISER AND OLDER THAN ME
HOW YOU TOUCHED MY HEART, THEN YOU RIPPED IT APART
YOU CHANGED AN INNOCENT SMILE, AND GIRLISH LAUGHTER
INTO CRYING EYES OVERNIGHT

CHORUS
SO GOOD LUCK, I HOPE YOU REALISE, WHAT I GAVE TO YOU
A VIRGIN'S LOVE, A CHILD'S TRUST,
MAKING LOVE WAS SOMETHING NEW
OH YOU FOUND ME SO YOUNG, AND TAUGHT ME ALL YOU KNEW
SO I'M LEAVING, A LOT WISER THAN YOU.

V2
I REMEMBER WHEN, I THOUGHT YOU WERE MY FRIEND
I BELIEVED ALL THOSE LIES YOU SAID, SHE DOESN'T UNDERSTAND
YOU'RE THE ONLY ONE FOR ME
SECRET RENDEZVOUS, STOLEN NIGHTS FOR TWO
THEN SUDDENLY SOMETHING HAPPENED AND I REALISED
I'D GIVEN IT ALL TO YOU

REPEAT CHORUS

Featured on If You Knew Suzi 1978

And again... from that same space in time. I had my career, I had my children, who were slowly growing up, and I was feeling lonely... see, there's that word again. Writing at this time gave me an escape from real life. I walked around in my own little world and would write until my kids returned from school... basically every single day, except when we were gigging. You can feel the need to escape in the lyrics.

Being alone in a relationship is the worst kind of lonely.

COMES THE NIGHT

(S. Quatro/Tuckey) Rak Pub.

V1
I'M DREAMING A DREAM IT'S SO SENSUAL
AN X RATED FANTASY
DEEP FEELING CONFUSING EMOTIONAL
MY MIND RACES TO BE FREE
OF THESE CHAINS, 'ROUND MY HEART
AND THIS POWER YOU GOT ON ME

CHORUS
COMES THE NIGHT, THE ANGEL OF LOVE IS BY MY SIDE
SHE'S BURNING BRIGHT,
MAKING THIS ROMANCE TURN OUT RIGHT
COMES THE NIGHT, COMES THE NIGHT

V2
SO LONELY I WANTED TO, NEEDED TO
BELIEVE IN A GENTLE TOUCH
SO HUNGRY LET ALL MY DEFENCES DOWN
ALLOWED YOU TO SEE TOO MUCH
OF MY HEART, BARED MY SOUL
ALL MY SECRETS, THE THINGS YOU KNOW

REPEAT CHORUS

BRIDGE
IT'S NOT JUST A GAME BUT HOW YOU PLAY IT
NOT HOW MUCH YOU LOVE, BUT HOW YOU SAY IT

REPEAT CHORUS

Recorded in 1983, released on Unreleased Emotions 1998

Yes, another around that time... all on the album Unreleased Emotions but written about 8 years earlier. I was feeling unfaithful in my mind constantly. I invented story lines of would-be lovers and affairs, and bought into them. Definitely mellow drama time!! Maybe instead of writing songs... we should have just talked... mmmm hindsight eh!!

And it must be said, the majority of these songs I wrote alone, which is obvious.

But I honoured our arrangement and our marriage. No regrets. These songs were written because of the situation I was in... so... to quote a song... all is fair in love and war.

This ended up on the album Oh Suzi Q... that I did with the Bolan Brothers.

• my second husband, Rainer Haas, married since 1993, and they said it wouldn't last.

BEST THING IN MY LIFE

(S. Quatro/Tuckey) Bellaphon

V1
SO MANY TIMES I TRIED TO WALK AWAY FROM YOU
EVERY TIME MY WINGS TOOK FLIGHT
MY RESTLESS HEART FLEW BACK TO YOU
YOU BELIEVED IN PERFECT LOVE, TO LAST ETERNALLY
HOW COULD I BETRAY A TRUST
A PERFECT LOVE I'D NEVER BE
JUST GOT TO TELL YOU I'M SORRY
I'VE JUST GOT TO MAKE YOU SEE

CHORUS
YOU'RE THE BEST THING IN MY LIFE
YOU'RE THE LIGHT SHINING IN MY EYES
YOU PUT THE MEANING BEHIND MY SMILE
YOU'RE THE BEST THING...... THE BEST THING IN MY LIFE

V2
SO MANY TEARS AND SLEEPLESS NIGHTS
GUESS IT'S HARD TO FACE THE TRUTH
TOO MANY YEARS, I CAN'T DENY IT
HAD NO RIGHT TO CHEAT ON YOU
JUST GOT TO TELL YOU I'M SO SORRY
GIMME ONE MORE CHANCE TO MAKE YOU SEE

REPEAT CHORUS

BRIDGE
WE'VE BOTH MADE MISTAKES, WE'VE HAD SOME REASON TO CRY
OHHH BUT WE GOT WHAT IT TAKES TO GET BY

REPEAT CHORUS

Featured on Oh Suzi Q, 1990

I met somebody around 1986, actually at one of the shows at Chichester of Annie Get Your Gun while I was playing Annie Oakley. Fantastic by the way... what a challenge. Eventually we became song writing partners and friends. She is still a friend. Another Gemini, so we clicked right away... all eight million of us.

And she came along when I was trying very hard to hold onto the remains of my marriage, which was disintegrating in front of my eyes. We wrote some really really good songs together sitting on the Chinese carpet in my front room, me with my bass, her with her acoustic guitar... pen and paper on the floor, small cassette recorder... creativity definitely still in the building. Maybe we will write again together... who knows... throwing that question out to the cosmos... And just a little footnote... I consider this the best bass riff I ever wrote... non negotiable.

And... all of our songs were after long discussions about life in general... this is how I work. As you will see through this book. Whoever I write 'with'... we need to discuss, dissect, and create the scenario... I am very open when I write... some would say... too open. Just the way I am wired.

WALKING THROUGH THE CHANGES

(S. Quatro/ R. Wolfe) Butterfly/Rak pub.

V1
WALKING THROUGH THE CHANGES FORGIVE AND FORTAKE
I'M A FLICKING THROUGH THE PAGES
FRIENDS TO FORSAKE
WHOOOO WHOA OH
THROUGH THE CHANGES OF LIFE

V2
HIT ME WITH YOUR HEAVY, NO TIME TO BE WRONG
DON'T NEED TO TALK SO HEAVY,
I'M TRAVELLING ON, WHOA.
THROUGH THE CHANGES OF LIFE
THROUGH THE CHANGES OF LIFE

CHORUS
I DON'T WANT TO TALK NO JIVE
I NEED TO KNOW, REALISE
THERE ARE THINGS THAT MONEY CAN'T BUY
THINGS THAT MONEY CAN'T BUY
I'VE SEEN PLEASURE THROUGH THE RAIN
DIG A LITTLE DEEPER THROUGH SUMMER PAIN
AH HA HA
WALK THROUGH THE CHANGES
YOU BETTER BELIEVE IT… GIMME A BREAK

Solo

REPEAT CHORUS

V3
HIT ME WITH YOUR HEAVY, NO TIME TO BE LONG
DON'T MEAN TO TALK SO HEAVY, I'M TRAVELLING ON
WHOA… THROUGH THE CHANGES OF LIFE,
THROUGH THE CHANGES OF LIFE

V4
WALKING THROUGH THE CHANGES FOR WHERE AND FOR HOW
I'M LIVING THROUGH THE PACES, STARTING FROM NOW
WHOA OH. THROUGH THE CHANGES OF LIFE
THROUGH THE CHANGES OF LIFE, AHHHHHHHH

Featured on The Girl From Detroit City, box set, Cherry Red Records 2014

I have a fond memory of composing this one. We were sitting on the floor as per normal. We started discussing this particular subject, creating a scenario, I came up with the title... which by the way is my forte... 'Elusive Lover'... then... I had to run and pick up the kids from school. I said to Rhiannon, keep working on this... I have a feeling the title should be in the very first line... to which she balked, loudly and said... oh no oh no... when I got back... the title was in the first line... AND the second line... Hahahahahahaha. When you're wrong you're wrong. Really good song, and when she sang backing vocals for a few years in my band, we actually did this as a duet, and... on Oh Suzi Q... it was recorded as a duet. The only one we ever did.

• Australian tour, last one with first husband, very stressful, circa 1990

ELUSIVE LOVER

(S. Quatro / R. Wolfe) Butterfly/Rak/Bellaphon

V1
SOMETIMES ELUSIVE LOVER
JUST ONE MORE TIME ELUSIVE LOVER
YOU'RE MY ONE DREAM REALITY
YOU'RE THE OTHER SIDE OF ME

V2
TOUCH ME ONE PERFECT MOMENT
THERE NEVER SEEMS TO BE THAT PERFECT MOMENT
YOU'RE COMPLETELY OUT OF REACH
YOU'RE THE DISAPPEARING FOOTPRINTS ON THE BEACH

CHORUS
WHY DO WE NEED WHAT WE NEVER CAN HAVE
IS YOUR BODY PLAYING GAMES WITH MY MIND
YOU ARE THE KEY TO THE PLEASURE IN SIDE
MY FANTASY, SEXUALITY
ELUSIVE LOVER, YOU'RE THE LOVE THAT NEVER CAN BE
ELUSIVE LOVER, YOU'RE MY FANTASY, NO MORALITY
ELUSIVE LOVER

V3
TELL ME, YOU BLAME ANOTHER
I NEVER MEANT TO BE UNCOVERED
SURRENDER YOUR SOUL TO ME
YOU'RE A NEVER ENDING CYCLE SET ME FREE

BRIDGE
WHEREVER YOU LEAD, (WHERE YOU WANDER)
I WILL FOLLOW BEHIND (I'LL STAY BY YOUR SIDE)
PERCHANCE TO DREAM (WILL YOU COME TO ME MY LOVE)
OH MY LOVE

REPEAT CHORUS

Featured on Oh Suzi Q, 1990

Another good song from the two of us. This idea came quite naturally: my son ran into the front room during a song writing session. He was going out to play, and I shouted after him 'kiss me goodbye'... ding ding ding... song title.

There is an existing Russian live concert, and it just pulls my heartstrings every time I see it... I come off stage... huge audience... sports stadium, sold out for 3 nights... 1989... and as I exit the stairs, 5-year-old Richard runs into my arms and hugs me tight. Guess at that age, he didn't like sharing me... understandable. And the other memory is... my daughter had learned the backing vocals and dance moves to this after watching us on t.v. and live after it was released and out on the market. She came into the front room one evening, put on the record and began to do the dance steps and sing the song... quite impressive... unfortunately her little brother came in and started to do his own version, which was terrible... jumping all over the place, screaming like a hooligan... we all, of course, started to laugh our asses off... Laura saw this, and immediately began to do the same thing as Richard.

Wonderful moments these.

KISS ME GOODBYE

(S. Quatro / R. Wolfe) Butterfly/Rak/Bellaphon

V1
I NEEDED YOU I COULDN'T FIND YOU WHOOO
I DIDN'T NEED YOU ANYMORE
YOU KNOW I WANTED YOU I COULDN'T SEE YOU WHOO
I DIDN'T HEAR YOU ANYMORE
WHOO WHOOOO
I'M GOING NOW, GOING NOW GOING NOW,
KISS ME GOODBYE

V2
DON'T KNOW WHAT YOU WANT ME TO BE
AND I DON'T CARE DOESN'T MATTER TO ME
BUT I CAN'T SHARE WITH SOMEONE WHO CAN'T SEE
HOW CAN YOU BE
SO COLD IN THE HEAT OF THE NIGHT WHEN IT'S
YOUR TURN HONEY, YOU GOT THE RIGHT BUT THERE'S
ONE THING BEFORE WE SAY GOODNIGHT

CHORUS
KISS ME GOODBYE, SO HARD I COULD DIE.. WHOOO
KISS ME GOODBYE

BRIDGE
FIND IT, TELL ME IF TRUTH HAS BEEN BLINDED
ONLY FOOLS HAVE TO HIDE IT
DOES THE JUSTICE FIT THE CRIME OF CONFUSION
OOO HOPELESS DELUSION
I'M GOING NOW, GOING NOW GOING NOW
KISS ME GOODBYE

REPEAT CHORUS

Featured on Oh Suzi Q 1990

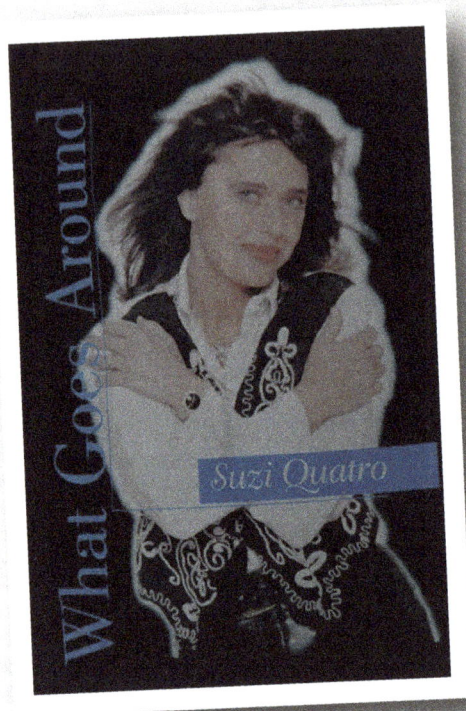

Okay... so do I have a favourite Quatro/Wolfe composition. Well, I guess this would be it. And again, after a long discussion on karma... big topic with me... big big big.

None of us gets away with anything... Good or bad... they both come back. This was the result. It is really really cool, a very unusual track... with talking... early rap perhaps. I have always maintained that you need an American accent to 'talk' on a record. Just my humble opinion. I remember recording this one for the now deleted re-recording of Latest and Greatest series on CMC. This song required bongos over the talking, and for some reason we decided Andy Dowding, my then drummer, should slap his knees... made a great sound actually... but poor Andy... this was years ago... I hope he has recovered.

• Karma is a wonderful thing, ad for album/single.

WHAT GOES AROUND

(S. Quatro / R. Wolfe) Butterfly/Rak/CMC

V1 (talk)
I WAS WALKING DOWN THE STREET,
SHOOK THE DUST FROM MY SHOES
THINKING OF A PLACE TO BE
I SAID HEY BABE, WE GOT NOTHING TO LOSE
THEY SAY THE BEST THINGS IN LIFE ARE FREE

CHORUS
WELL DON'T YOU KNOW THAT WHAT GOES AROUND
COMES AROUND, AND WHAT GOES AROUND
COMES AROUND, IT GOES ROUND AND ROUND
AND ROUND AND ROUND AND ROUND

V2
EVERYONE CAN BE CRUEL SOMETIMES
IT'S A LONELY LIFE, SUCH A LONELY LIFE
WHEN YOU TAKE WHAT YOU NEED
LOVE IS THE SEED, ON WHICH WE FEED

REPEAT CHORUS

V3
AND I WILL TAKE YOU THERE ON A MYSTICAL FLIGHT
AND WE'LL MAKE IT THERE AND IT WILL BE ALRIGHT
AND YOU CAN CALL ME CRAZY (YOU'RE CRAZY)
CALL ME CRAZY WE'LL BE LAUGHIN' WALKING, SWEET TALKING

REPEAT CHORUS

V4 (talk)
YOU AND ME BABE, YEAH WE GOT WHAT IT TAKES
WE DON'T LIVE FOR LIFE NO, NOT FOR LOVE'S SAKE
LONELY NIGHTS LONELY NIGHTS
LONELY LONELY.. LONE……

REPEAT CHORUS

Featured on What Goes Around 1996

And another discussion, drinking coffee, discussing life and all its pitfalls. Oh boy, Geminis can go the distance for hours and hours and hours... and then, they are silent. This was a long moment for us.

It's all about catching somebody's eye at a party. It all happens within milliseconds, the entire scenario plays across your mind, you can see everything, you know what they look like making love to you, you know what you will feel like making love to them, you can smell it, feel it, touch it... it is real... and then... it's gone. And we have all been there.

Question... we have all been there... what stops us from doing something about it? Answer... the fantasy is always better than the reality... maybe???

INTIMATE STRANGERS

(S. Quatro / R. Wolfe) Butterfly/Rak/Bellaphon

V1
EYE TO EYE ACROSS A CROWDED ROOM
YOU CHANGED MY LIFE, YOU CHANGED MY LIFE
SMILE TO SMILE, AS WOULD BE LOVERS DO
UNCHAIN MY LIFE, UNCHAIN MY LIFE

V2
FACE TO FACE YOU SEEM SO FAR AWAY
A SILENT WORD, UNSILENT WORD
YOU TOUCH MY HAND AND THE MUSIC DIES AWAY
BUT NO-ONE HEARD, DIDN'T ANYONE HEAR, THE SOUND OF

CHORUS
MELODY, IN POETRY, OF INTIMATE STRANGERS
YOU AND I, ONE PASSING MOMENT IN OUR LIVES
IT'S JUST A HEAVENLY, PARODY
OF INTIMATE STRANGERS, IN THE NIGHT
YOU SAILED MY HEART AWAY
SO INTIMATE, TOO INTIMATE, THE WHISPERS OF STRANGERS
INTIMATE STRANGERS

V3
CARESSING THOUGHTS AS THEY TURN THE LIGHTS DOWN LOW
TOO SOFT TO SHOW, TOO CLOSE TO KNOW
YOU BRUSHED MY LIPS, THE FEELING WAS ENOUGH
ONE TOUCH TOO MUCH, COULD MEAN SO MUCH
(YOU SAILED MY HEART AWAY) YOU SAILED MY HEART AWAY

REPEAT CHORUS

EYE TO EYE ACROSS A CROWDED ROOM
A CLOSING SCENE
DARE WE TO DREAM

Featured on The Girl From Detroit City, box set, 2014

This one never actually got recorded properly and exists only on tape. I used to have a recording studio up on the third floor at this time, which eventually became the nanny's, and gardener's quarters, and also for a long time, once I had no live-in home help, became my son's bedroom... it has finally become exactly what it should always have been, my 'ego' room. I have put this song in here because I really like the lyrics very much. And... this is about somebody... well, let's just say this person was the blueprint... artistic licence and all that.

• Dee on left, such a talent, r.i.p. my friend.

LET IT DIE

(S. Quatro / R. Wolfe) Butterfly/Rak

V1
CLINGING TO SOMETHING
YOU CAN NEVER HAVE
HANGING ON TO A MISPLACED DREAM
YOU'RE TRYING FOR SOMETHING,
YOU TRIED SO HARD TO BE
OOOOO, BUT YOU CAN NEVER BE ME

V2
LYING TO SOMEONE
DO YOU CRY ALONE
HOLDING ON TO A MAKE BELIEVE
A FADED PICTURE, OF A FADING MEMORY
DON'T YOU SEE , DON'T YOU SEE
YOU COULD NEVER BE ME
YOUR SELFISH OBSESSION

CHORUS
WHY DON'T YOU.. LET IT DIE
LET IT DIE , CUZ THERE IS NO MORE
OH LET IT DIE, I CAN CARRY YOU NO MORE

V3
REACHING FOR SOMEONE
TAKING ALL IN SHAME
BREAKING DOWN WHEN I WASN'T THERE
DID YOU EVER NEED ME
HOW COULD YOU BELIEVE
YOU COULD EVER BE ME
I AN NOT YOUR POSSESSION

REPEAT CHORUS

YOUR SELFISH OBSESSION

REPEAT CHORUS

Demo, never released

Without a doubt... one of my best compositions, in my top 5. These kind of songs come along once in a lifetime... when life's sadness knocks you over like a freight train. Your emotions take complete control, you open your mind, your heart, your soul, sit at the piano, guitar to hand, pen, paper... open the channels and just let it flow. I wrote this because I didn't know how to tell my ex-husband I wanted to leave the marriage... I thought this song would do the job for me... in a kind, hopeful way. Didn't work.

But no matter how painful it all was/still is, it created a real piece of magic.

FREE THE BUTTERFLY

(S. QUATRO) Butterfly/Rak

V1
ONE KISS FOR YESTERDAY,
ONE HOPE FOR TOMORROW
FACE TO FACE WITH SORROW
NOTHING LEFT TO SAY
ONE MORE LOVE AFFAIR DEAD AND GONE
TWO WEARY CONTENDERS, MOVING ON
WILL THE SNAKE SHED ITS SKIN
WHEN THE TRUTH RUSHES IN

CHORUS
SO LET THE CHRYSALIS BEGIN
FREE THE BUTTERFLY WITHIN
SPREAD MY WINGS, I WANNA FLY
AND LET MY HAPPINESS BEGIN
FREE THE BUTTERFLY WITHIN
SPREAD MY WINGS, JUST GOT TO TRY
FREE THIS BUTTERFLY…FREE…….THIS BUTTERFLY

V2
PRECIOUS MOMENTS
WE CAN'T FORGET
A PROMISE FOREVER
YES KNOW THAT IT'S OVER
MY HEART HAS NO REGRET
CUZ THE LOVE WE SHARED
HAS FLOWN AWAY
ALTHOUGH I'M BESIDE YOU EVERYDAY
WE SHARED THE BEST
NOW IT'S TIME TO PUT THIS PAIN TO REST

REPEAT CHORUS

BRIDGE
THE SNAKE SHEDS ITS SKIN, TRUTH RUSHES IN
I START TO CRY… THIS IS GOODBYE

REPEAT CHORUS

Featured on Back to the Drive, 2006

So leading nicely into the next 'divorce' stage of my life, and creative wise, well, judge for yourselves. I had a very lost year (all in Unzipped)... Feeling 'lonely'... whoops... there's that word again... I really love the lyrics of this next one. It delves into how we can relax with someone we care about... truly relax... and really show who we are, especially in bed, where we are... naked!! Both in clothes, and emotionally, and if you are not naked both these ways... sorry... but it's not love... most likely lust... which is okay too. There is a wonderful clip of me doing this as a duet with my daughter Laura. Brings a tear to my eye every time I see it.

• Had a good day, not my normal look, knew it would be a good session.

AND SO TO BED

(S. Quatro) Butterfly/Rak

V1
WHEN YOU'RE TIRED OF BEING STRONG
SO TIRED OF SINGING THAT SAME OLD SONG
OH.. YOU'VE GOT TO REACH OUT
WHEN YOUR MIND GOES ALL INSANE
CAUGHT IN THE EYE OF LIFE'S HURRICANE
OH.. YOU'VE GOT TO REACH AND TOUCH SOMEBODY
(REACH OUT) YOU'VE GOT TO LOVE SOMEBODY
OOOO OOOO SOMEBODY

CHORUS
AND SO TO BED, WHERE THE LIGHTS ARE LOW
CHASING SHADOWS, CROSS MY PILLOW
AND SO TO BED, WHERE I GO TO SHOW
ALL THE COLOURS OF MY RAINBOW
SO TO BED

V2
WHEN ALL THE WORLD LOOKS WRONG
YOU CAN'T REMEMBER WHERE YOU BELONG
OH.. YOU'VE GOT TO REACH OUT
AND TOUCH SOMEBODY (REACH OUT)
YOU'VE GOT TO LOVE SOMEBODY
OO OO OO

BRIDGE
AND IF YOUR HEART'S BEEN LOST AND LONELY FOR AWHILE
I KNOW A PLACE, A SPACE FOR LOVERS ONLY

CHORUS
AND SO TO BED, TO BED WHERE THE LIGHTS ARE LOW
MAKING SHADOWS CROSS MY PILLOW
TO BED WHERE I GO TO SHOW ALL THE COLOURS
OF MY RAINBOW AND SO TO BED

Released as B-side, 1993, Germany only, of 'Fear of the Unknown',
also featured on The Girl From Detroit City box set, 2014

Some moments are captured in your mind's eye forever.
I had just picked up the kids from school, it had been
raining and I saw the most spectacular rainbow in front
of us. Pulled over and just looked at it for a minute, then
said to Laura and Richard, who were strapped in, in the
back seat, 'Why do rainbows always have to die?'
I remember the silence in the car. We went home, the
kids ran up to change their school clothes and go out and
play, and I went straight to my 'creating' room and
wrote this song.

It was one of those that simply flew out, piano, melody
and lyrics, like it had already been written. Strange as
well, there is no actual chorus, and there doesn't need to
be... it just rolled out as it should.

It was also one of the songs I did with Mickie Most on
the last sessions we ever did together.
Fitting, don't you think?

WHY DO RAINBOWS DIE

(S. QUATRO) Butterfly/Rak Pub

V1
I SAW A RAINBOW, BEAUTIFUL RAINBOW
THEN IT FADED AWAY
I SAW OUR DREAMS GO, BELOW ZERO
TILL THE WIND JUST BLEW THEM AWAY
ELECTRIC STORMS LIGHT UP OUR LIVES
THEN THE CALM ARRIVES
AND THE COLOURS SHINE DOWN SOFTLY FROM THE SKY
TELL ME WHY DO RAINBOWS ALWAYS HAVE TO DIE

V2
I FELT THE OCEAN, MOVE MY EMOTION
THE WAVES ROLLED IN SO GENTLY
BLUE SEA WAS CALLING, AS I WAS FALLING
INTO A VOID OF ECSTASY
I TRIED TO SWIM AGAINST MY TIDE
I TRIED TO DROWN MY FEARS INSIDE
I WAS DESPERATE TO REACH THE OTHER SIDE
BUT WHEN I LOOKED UP I SAW THE RAINBOW DIE

BRIDGE
WE THOUGHT OUR STARS WOULD ALWAYS SHINE
TOGETHER, TILL THE END OF TIME
I THOUGHT THAT YOU'D BE MINE FOREVER MORE AND

V3
I SAW A RAINBOW, BEAUTIFUL RAINBOW
BUT IT FADED AWAY
I SAW OUR DREAMS GO, BELOW ZERO
TILL THE WIND JUST BLEW THEM AWAY
ELECTRIC STORMS LIGHT UP OUR LIVES
THEN THE CALM ARRIVES
WHY DO LOVERS ALWAYS SAY GOODBYE
TELL ME WHY DO RAINBOWS ALWAYS HAVE TO DIE
WHY DO LOVERS ALWAYS HAVE TO CRY
WHY DO RAINBOWS ALWAYS HAVE TO DIE

Bonus track on Unreleased Emotion 1998

This song goes deep down... very very deep down. When a marriage breaks up, no matter who does the leaving, it is heartbreaking. My first marriage finished. We decided to do the actual moving of some of the furniture he would be taking to his new home while I was on tour in Japan, with the two kids, so they would not have to be witness to it. I came home to empty rooms. It was so sad to see the spaces where pieces of furniture used to be, like the spaces in my heart where the love used to be. I wandered around looking, touching, remembering, and crying. Finally I sat at my piano, and composed this. It remains one of the most poignant things I ever wrote in my life. I lived every word.

I did this on stage for a couple of years. Much as I love the song it was always a little hard to sing.

• My face says it all, ...I have always been transparent.

EMPTY ROOMS

(S. Quatro) Butterfly/CMC Int.

V1
DO YOU CALL THIS LOVE,
WHEN HEARTACHE IS THE ONLY SOUND I HEAR
LONELY FOOTSTEPS ECHO
A DREAM LOST IN TIME
HOW CAN I EXPLAIN
MY FEELINGS, WHEN MY BACK'S AGAINST THE WALL
HOW CAN I STAY SANE WHEN
I'VE NEARLY LOST MY MIND
WHY CAN'T YOU SEE,
WHAT THIS MASQUERADE IS DOING TO YOU AND ME

CHORUS
EMPTY ROOMS, EMPTY ROOMS
FILLED WITH SADNESS, AND STALE PERFUME
WE KNEW IT WENT WRONG, FOR MUCH TOO LONG
YES WE TOOK A RIDE ON A FAIRYTALE
BUT NOW THAT FAIRYTALE IS THROUGH

V2
HOW CAN YOU DENY, YOUR ANGER
IT'S BURNING IN YOUR EYES
HOW CAN WE SURVIVE IT, THIS HOLOCAUST TONIGHT
DO YOU THINK THAT BLAME, CAN SAVE YOU
FROM LOOKING IN YOUR SOUL
DO YOU CALL IT SHAMEFUL COZ
I REFUSE TO FIGHT

BRIDGE
BUT I LOVED YOU, YOU KNOW IT'S TRUE
I REALLY LOVED YOU, BUT WE
CAN'T IGNORE THIS LOVE AND WAR
EACH TIME WE WALK IN TO

REPEAT CHORUS

Featured on What Goes Around 1996

1993, I got married for the second time. At the time of writing this lyric book we are in our 27th year together. Not bad for a girl!! When we first got together, and as all new couples do, we shared our stories. He told me his story of the girlfriend before me, and that they had 9 years together, then had split up for a year, then got back together for another year, which was a mistake because the same problems started all over again, which eventually killed his love for her.

I found that interesting artistically, and came up with this song.

ONE DANCE TOO LONG

(S. QUATRO) Butterfly/Rak Pub

V1
THERE WAS NOTHING I COULD DO
CUZ I LOST MYSELF IN YOU
I HAD A DREAM, A LOVER'S FANTASY
PAINTING A SCENE OF HOW I WISHED IT COULD BE

V2
DID SHE TRULY MAKE YOU CRY
DID YOU FALL, AND NOT KNOW WHY
YOU WERE SO LOST INSIDE YOUR LONELINESS
YOU COULDN'T SEE THE ROAD TO HAPPINESS

CHORUS
YOU DANCED ONE DANCE TOO LONG
RELYING ON A MELODY TO
CARRY US ALONG
BUT WHO CAN DANCE TO A SILENT SYMPHONY

V3
WHEN THE PROMISES YOU MAKE
ARE THE VERY ONES YOU BREAK
DO YOU RETURN ONCE MORE TO FANTASY
OR CAN YOU BELIEVE IN OUR REALITY

REPEAT CHORUS

Featured as a bonus track on Unreleased Emotion 1998

I had this riff for quite a while... being a riff type muso anyway. I got the title first...

Then I painted the scene. Picture the dude, cowboy boots, cowboy hat, skintight jeans, sleeveless t-shirt... muscles on show... wanders into the café at the truck stop, where you have decided to take a little coffee break from your long solo drive across country. He sashays to the corner table, orders a beer and a sandwich, and your eyes lock. The deal is made in that one moment. And to steal a line from my favourite movie of all time, All About Eve... 'Fasten your seat belts, its going to be a bumpy night.'

This one made it to the stage too, but we didn't play it very often. It is a musician's song, so I am told.

• Biker, rock chick with bass, enquire inside.

TRUCK STOP

(S. QUATRO) Butterfly/Rak Pub

V1
HE SAID, IT'S COMMITMENT TIME
AND YET, HE SIDE STEPS THE RHYME (YOU KNOW WHAT I MEAN)
HE'S GOT A FOUR WHEEL DRIVE DOWN A DUSTY ROAD
WINDSHIELD WIPERS, BEATING THE TIME BACK HOME
(I GOTTA TELL YOU NOW)

V2
YOU PAY A HIGH PRICE FOR LOVE
YOU PUSH REAL HARD, BUT YOU FORGOT TO SHOVE
ANOTHER CHEAP HOTEL DOWN A DEAD END STREET
GOT THE BLUES, GOT THE BIBLE
AND BOTH OF THEM GOT ME BEAT

CHORUS
HERE AT THE TRUCK STOP
THERE AIN'T NO QUESTIONS ASKED
HERE AT THE TRUCK STOP
ALL YOU NEED IS (A POCKETFUL OF CASH)

BRIDGE
YES IT'S BEEN A LONELY RIDE, BUT I GUESS THAT'S ROCK N ROLL
CAFFEINE HIGH DRIVES THROUGH THE NIGHT
CUZ YOU GOTTA LONG WAY TO GO
YOU CAN'T HIDE FROM ANYTHING
WHEN YOU'RE MILES AWAY FROM SANE
HANG OUT LOOSE IN YOUR WANDERING SHOES
TILL YOU WALK AWAY THE PAIN

V3
I'M ON THE COLD SIDE OF HELL
TOO OLD TO BE YOUNG ENOUGH TO SELL
(YOU KNOW WHAT I MEAN)
I GOT HIGH HEELED BOOTS AND SNAKESKIN EYES
I'M A MEAN MAD MAMA, AND I CAN CUT YOU DOWN TO SIZE.

REPEAT CHORUS

Featured on In the Spotlight deluxe CD, In the Dark, 2012

Another one from the last recording sessions I did with Mickie Most. I had this song for a while and had demoed it with my normal band... good demo too.

I particularly like the lyrics on this. Tells the story of somebody who has enough smarts to call a spade a spade, and enough balls to go out and follow their dream... now who do you think that somebody is?? The question is rhetorical.

AMBITION

(S. Quatro) Butterfly/Rak Pub

V1
I WAS HANGING 'ROUND IN A DEAD END TOWN
WHERE DREAMS DIE
AND THE ONLY SOUND WAS THE ECHO OF
GOODBYE IN MY MIND
I SAW MY CHOICES BECKON, LIKE GOLD DUST IN THE SKY
SO I PACKED UP MY LIFE, LEFT MY HEART BEHIND
WAS A HEAVY RIDE, WITH A SUITCASE
FULL OF MEMORIES
GOT A PICTURE OF YOU
AND A VISION OF NEW HORIZONS TO FLY
I THOUGHT I HAD TO ANSWER
TO THIS EMPTINESS INSIDE
BUT I GUESS FAME IS JUST
ANOTHER PLACE TO HIDE

CHORUS
AMBITION, IT'S A FUNNY OLD GAME
AMBITION, DRIVES A GIRL INSANE
BUT MONEY TALKS, AND FAILURE WALKS ALONE
AMBITION, WALK HER INTO THE FIRE
AMBITION, SHE NEEDS A SHOT OF DESIRE
SO SOME POOR FOOL, LIKE ME AND YOU CAN FOLLOW
INTO THE LIGHT

V2
IT'S A HEAVY ROAD, WHEN YOU THINK
YOU'RE GOING NOWHERE
AND THE FUTURE HOLDS ALL THE SAME MISTAKES
YOU TRIED TO IGNORE
MY MAMA TRIED TO WARN ME
BUT I SAID I DID NOT CARE
I WAS FIFTEEN PUSHING THIRTY, HEADING OUT THAT DOOR

CHORUS

BRIDGE
SHE WAS BORN TO DANCE IN THE SPOTLIGHT
CUZ THE FEELING INSIDE IS SO RIGHT, TONIGHT SO RIGHT HEY HEY
HEY

CHORUS

Featured as bonus track on Unreleased Emotion 1998

After marrying for the second time, my writing took on a completely different quality.

Having been through the emotional wringer of a very very painful divorce, coming out the other side, and finding happiness again, I was able to delve into these areas with a certain amount of safety. Let's just say, my creativity took true flight from this moment onwards. I feel unencumbered, free, artistic, able to soar to the heights with nobody to hold me down. Not that there ever was, it just felt like there was. Since this period of my life began up to the present day I am loving writing songs more than ever... and never seem to run out of ideas. I am like a radio receptor tuned into the right channel, and believe me, I will stay tuned in. This next one is what I consider one of my finest numbers. I have always wanted to do this as a duet. Maybe one day this will come true; it's on my bucket list.

• *it's all in the eyes*

IF THERE EVER WAS A REASON

(S. Quatro) Butterfly/Rak Pub

V1
IF THERE EVER WAS REASON FOR LOVING YOU
YOU GAVE IT TO ME TONIGHT
IT'S THE WAY THAT YOU TOUCH ME IN ALL OF THOSE PLACES
NO-ONE ELSE GETS RIGHT
SO LET'S PLAY THE MUSIC
DRINK THE WINE
I STILL NEED A LITTLE TIME TO MAKE UP
MY WANDERING MIND

CHORUS
AND IF THERE EVER WAS A REASON
IF THERE EVER WAS A REASON
IF THERE EVER WAS A REASON FOR LOVING YOU
YOU GAVE IT TO ME TONIGHT, OH OH, YOU GAVE IT TO ME
TONIGHT

V2
WELL YOU KNOCKED ON THE DOOR OF MY EMPTY HEART
THOUGHT I MIGHT LET YOU IN
AND IT'S BEEN TOO DAMN LONG I'VE BEEN LIVING SO LONELY
SO HOW DO I BEGIN
CAN YOU READ THE POEMS, SING THE SONGS
I STILL NEED A LITTLE TIME TO WORK OUT
WHERE I BELONG

REPEAT CHORUS

BRIDGE
AND IF I SHOULD ASK YOU, INTO MY LIFE
(I WANT TO BE ALL THE REASONS
SO THAT YOU CAN BELIEVE IT MY LOVE)
COULD YOU BE MY SAVIOUR, MY WHITE KNIGHT
(JUST TAKE A CHANCE WITH ME,
WE COULD DANCE INTO ETERNITY)

REPEAT CHORUS

Featured on In the Spotlight deluxe CD, In the Dark 2012,
also featured on The Girl From Detroit City box set, 2014

So continuing along these lines of thought emotionally, this is about one of those situations we all maybe have or maybe will find ourselves in. We really like somebody and want to go the distance, this other person likes us too but is reluctant to actually consummate the relationship... very frustrating all round. Need drives the woman, fear drives the man... not a good concept but made a good song.

Did this onstage for awhile in the early 90s. Had a horn section by then so this was perfect. I treated the arrangement along the same lines as Otis Redding's 'Try A Little Tenderness', one of my favourite recordings of all time.

MAKE LOVE TO ME

(S. Quatro) Butterfly/Rak

V1
WELL I TRIED TO SPEAK MY THOUGHTS
BUT THEY CAME OUT ALL WRONG
AND I TRIED TO SLOW THINGS DOWN
BUT IT WAS MUCH TOO STRONG
I COULD ALWAYS SEE THE TRUTH WITHIN THE LIES
AS THE PASSION BURNED ANOTHER HOLE IN YOUR DISGUISE

V2
SEEDS OF LUST WILL ALWAYS FIND A SPACE TO GROW
SCARED, IS JUST ANOTHER WORD, FOR CAN'T LET GO
SO I BEG YOU RECONSIDER JUST FOR TONIGHT
CUZ I AIN'T NO QUITTER, I WON'T LOSE AND I GOT YOU IN MY SIGHT

CHORUS
MAKE LOVE TO ME, SWEET LOVE TO ME
I'LL BE IN EVERY DREAM THAT YOU DREAM
I'LL BE YOUR EVERYTHING, IF YOU,
MAKE LOVE TO ME

V3
IF THE DEVIL THAT YOU KNOW
CAN'T KEEP YOU SATISFIED
ARE THE NEEDS YOU SHOW THE VERY NEEDS
THAT YOU DENIED
I'M NOT ASKING YOU TO WANT ME FOREVER MORE
BUT I'M ASKING YOU TO SHOW ME
WHAT THESE EMPTY ARMS ARE FOR

BRIDGE
ONLY TIME WILL TELL THE TRUTH ABOUT YOU AND ME
ONLY TIME, ONLY TIME, WILL FINALLY LET US BE.. SO FREE
SO MAKE LOVE MAKE LOVE MAKE LOVE

REPEAT CHORUS

Featured on In the Spotlight deluxe CD, In the Dark 2012

Sorry, but you can't actually hear this song anywhere... YET... I don't know why I am saving it but I am. It only exists in demo form. It's a winner, one of Shirlie Roden's and my best collaborations.

It is quite theatrical and would be great in a musical, or a movie, maybe that's what I am waiting for. You know the moment, you meet somebody, completely unexpected, and you do that dance in each other's eyes. Chemistry, lust, love, who the hell knows what to call it. The only thing I am sure of is it exists... and it is so powerful. In fact, that's what I love about this feeling: you have zero control... and me being the control freak I am I find it irresistible. And a little bit dangerous... to be continued.

• Sold it out, 2017.. wow wow wow...

IF THE WORLD WAS RIGHT

(S.Quatro/Shirlie Roden) Butterfly/Rak Pub./Singing Earth music Ltd.

V1
I COULD FALL INTO YOUR EYES FOREVER,
AND NEVER NEED TO KNOW
THE REASON WHY WE'VE BEEN THROWN TOGETHER
BUT I JUST CAN'T LET THIS MOMENT GO
YOU SAY THINGS LIKE THIS DON'T HAPPEN, IT JUST DID
LET'S DENY IT WALK AWAY RIGHT NOW,
SO WHO WE TRYING TO KID

CHORUS
AND IF THE WORLD WAS RIGHT I'D LAY BESIDE YOU
IF THE GAME WAS OURS TO PLAY
AND IF WE HAD ONE NIGHT, I COULD BARELY STOP
IF THE WORLD WAS RIGHT…. BUT IT'S NOT

V2
WHEN I LOOKED INTO YOUR SOUL FOREVER,
I KNEW I'D NEVER LOVED BEFORE
I LOST ALL MY CONTROL, AND I DON'T KNOW WHETHER
I CAN FIND THE STRENGTH TO CLOSE THIS OPEN DOOR
WE SPOKE A THOUSAND WORDS WE CAN'T RECALL
BUT THE MORE WE TRY TO PULL AWAY
THE HARDER WE BOTH FALL

CHORUS
AND IF THE WORLD WAS RIGHT I'D LAY BESIDE YOU
IF THE GAME WAS OURS TO PLAY
AND IF WE HAD ONE NIGHT I COULD BARELY STOP
BUT WE DIDN'T MAKE THE RULES, WE ARE DESTINY'S FOOLS
NO NO WE CAN'T BREAK THE RULES , IT JUST AIN'T FAIR.

AND IF WE HAD ONE NIGHT,
I COULD BARELY STOP,
IF THE WORLD WAS RIGHT

REPEAT CHORUS

Demo only, never released yet.

This is an interesting story. I met an older man in Australia, a very known radio personality.

He interviewed me on his t.v. show. We hit it off from the moment we met. I found him very interesting and intelligent... and he found me the same. I liked him... a lot. We had a wonderful interview, very warm, very natural, and then parted. When I got back to my hotel, I felt the need to write this song, and I knew it was about him. I have no idea why. I didn't really even know him. But, a few months later, every word in this song came true. Don't ask me to explain it... I can't... but I do know it happened.

Synergy, chemistry, prophecy... whatever you want to call it... it happened.

DANCING IN THE WIND

(S. Quatro/S.Roden) Butterfly/Rak/Singing Earth Music ltd.

V1
IN YOUR GLASS MENAGERIE YOU HIDE
YOU CAN'T FACE THE DAY, KIND OF DEAD INSIDE
DOWN AGAIN FROM YOUR EGO HIGH AND MIGHTY
WHERE ILLUSION PLAYS IN BETWEEN THE LIES
AND YOU LOOK SO VAIN WITH YOUR SNAKESKIN EYES
ANAESTHETISING MORALISING TO SURVIVE
OHHH.. AIN'T LIFE FUNNY

V2
AS THE CRITICS BITE AND THE CAMERAS FLASH
THE WOLVES ARE HUNGRY FOR YOU TO CRASH
PICKING ON EVERY SINGLE THING YOU SAY
THEY TRY TO PUT YOU DOWN YOU'RE STILL TALKING FREE
YOU WON'T SHOW YOUR VULNERABILITY
TO THE PAPARAZZI CIRCLING THE PREY
OHHH. AIN'T LIFE FUNNY
HOW A LITTLE TOO MUCH OF TRUTH CAN GET YOU DOWN

CHORUS
AND IT'S SO DAMN LONELY, IN A WORLD SO PHONEY
WHERE THE CHEATERS NEVER KNOWN THEY'VE SINNED
WILL YOUR WINGS KEEP FLYING, THROUGH THE LOST HORIZON
HAS YOUR SPIRIT GONE DANCING IN THE WIND

V3
SHINY SUIT AND TIE , LIFE'S A COMPROMISE
THE LION ROARS AS THE JUNGLE CRIES
FOOLS YOU'VE SUFFERED, DAMN THEM ALL TO HELL
AS THE GAMES EXPOSED THEY CAN FEEL YOUR STING
AS THE WEAKEST FALLS TO THE POWER KING
THEY JUST DON'T UNDERSTAND, YOU'VE TAKEN EVERYTHING
OHHH, AIN'T LIFE FUNNY
HOW REALITY CREEPS IN WITHOUT A SOUND

REPEAT CHORUS

Featured on Back to the Drive 2006

This exists only on a demo. Depending on the project,
everything must slot in. This one didn't fit. I love the song and
the lyric, but perhaps... the entire situation, just didn't fit.
Someday I will record this properly, in the meantime, you
have to be content with just the lyrics. With or without
music... it paints the picture, and is extremely poetic... and dare
I say... romantic... let your imagination fly.

• recording aborted album

IT ALL LEADS BACK TO YOU

(S.Quatro) Butterfly/Rak

V1
RAINDROPS ON MY WINDOWSILL
PASSING STRANGERS SMILE
LOVERS 'NEATH A PALE MOONLIGHT,
SAILING DOWN THE NILE
DANCERS IN THE TWILIGHT
RHAPSODY IN BLUE
OUR SONG IN A SMALL CAFÉ
SYMPHONY FOR TWO
AND I'VE BEEN FEELING DOWN
FELLING LOW
I'VE BEEN LOOKING ROUND
WHICH WAY SHOULD I GO

V2
FRENCH KISSES IN A MOVIE SHOW
BAREFOOT IN THE SAND
CHOPIN ON THE STEREO, HOLDING HAND IN HAND
LOVE LETTERS IN A MAGAZINE
DON'T EVER SAY ADIEU
ROMANCE ON THE RADIO,
THIS IS DEDICATED TO

CHORUS
AND I'VE BEEN FEELING DOWN, FEELING LOW
I'M BEEN LOOKING ROUND, WHICH WAY SHOULD I GO
AND I'VE BEEN FEELING DOWN, FEELING LOW
CUZ IT ALL LEADS BACK TO YOU
WHAT AM I SUPPOSED TO DO

V3
POETRY AT SUNSET, CHAMPAGNE BY THE FIRE
SONNETS IN A PHOTOGRAPHY, PICTURES OF DESIRE
DANCERS IN THE TWILIGHT, RHAPSODY IN BLUE
OUR SONG IN A SMALL CAFÉ, SYMPHONY FOR TWO

CHORUS

Demo only never released

This is, I believe, Shirlie Roden's and my very best song together, along with, 'If the World Was Right'... We hit the mark on both.

I was telling her the story of my mother's last healthy trip to the UK. She had stomach cancer and would not live very long. We took a lot of very slow walks around the house where I live. I knew I would not be able to talk again to her, not at this level. So I talked and talked and asked a million questions. On one particular walk, she got very quiet... her steps were very slow because she was just not healthy anymore. She said to me... 'I let you go too early, much too early, you joined that damn rock and roll band... too young... just too young...' We walked in silence a little more, then I replied, 'Mom, why didn't you just say no?' And her reply was 'Because my Susan, sometimes love is letting go.' I knew one day it would be a song.

This was the closing song in my one woman show, Unzipped, in 2014. Although it came from my mother's comment, when we wrote it, it became something much more. It hasn't actually got an official chorus, but instead, tells the story in 3 parts.

SOMETIMES LOVE IS LETTING GO

(S. Quatro/S. Roden) Butterfly/Rak/Singing Earth Music ltd.

(spoken)
MY MAMA ALWAYS TOLD ME, IF YOU TRULY LOVE SOMEONE, DON'T
HOLD ON TOO TIGHT, SOMETIMES LOVE IS LETTING GO

V1
SOMETIMES LOVE IS LETTING GO,
YOU'VE FALLEN HARD, EVEN THOUGH
HE SHOWS YOU NOTHING, IN RETURN
BUT YOU STILL GIVE EVERYTHING
CUZ YOU'VE YET TO LEARN
THAT IF HE'S YOURS, ONE DAY HE'LL KNOW
SOMETIMES LOVE IS LETTING GO

(spoken)
YOU KNOW MY DAD ALWAYS TOLD ME, THAT MEN DON'T SHOW
THEIR FEELINGS EASY, SO I SAID, HEY DAD, THE TIMES I'VE SEEN YOU
CRY ARE THE MOST PRECIOUS TO ME

V2
SOMETIMES LOVE IS LETTING GO
AND WHEN YOU'RE SCARED, SCARED TO LET LOVE SHOW
AND SO AFRAID, YOUR HEART WILL BREAK
JUST LET IT HAPPEN, FOR YOUR LOVE'S SAKE
SWEET EMOTION, YOU GOT TO LET IT FLOW
SOMETIMES LOVE IS LETTING GO

(spoken)
AND WHEN I FINALLY GREW UP, I FELL IN LOVE, BUT IT DIDN'T LAST,
WE JUST DIDN'T BELONG TOGETHER ANYMORE, AND I HAD TO BE
STRONG AND SAY TO MYSELF, HEY GIRL,
SOMETIMES LOVE IS LETTING GO

V3
SOMETIMES LOVE, IS LETTING GO
WE WERE FLYING HIGH, NOW WE'RE LYING LOW
IN YOUR ARMS LIKE A STRANGER, YOU FEEL SO COLD
THE TRUTH IS PLAIN, BUT RARELY TOLD
YOU GOTTA STOP SAYING YES, WHEN YOU MEAN NO
AND IF HE'S YOURS SOME DAY HE'LL KNOW
SWEET EMOTION, YOU GOTTA LET IT FLOW
CUZ SOMETIMES LOVE.. IS LETTING GO

Featured on Back to the Drive 2006

Well, the story has been told over and over again, every newspaper, every t.v. show, they all bring this up. So... here, I hope for the last time, is the story. I was in the U.S.A. on tour, 1974, my version of 'All Shook Up' was out and was in the lower end of the charts... I was in Memphis, the phone rang, it was Elvis' people, then he got on the phone... as you can imagine I nearly died. He said, 'I heard your version of "All Shook Up" and I think it's the best since my own, and I would like to invite you to Graceland...' I said, 'I'm very busy'... groans all around... I can hear you. Truth is, I simply was not quite ready to meet him... not scared, just not quite ready. And my path was to write this song. If I had met him, my feelings would have been different and this song would not exist... this song had to exist. It is now done by Elvis impersonators around the world, and sung at funerals. I recorded this in Nashville, with James Burton on guitar, and the Jordanaires. Andy Scott was producing. My Elvis cycle was complete at last.

• first photo, hubby, Glen Harding, me, James Burton, a huge Elvis show we did, second photo, Graceland - file this under perspective.

SINGING WITH ANGELS

(S.Quatro) Butterfly/Rak

V1
I HEARD YOUR VOICE LATE LAST NIGHT
I HEARD YOU SAY ARE YOU LONESOME TONIGHT
I SAW YOU CRYING IN THE CHAPEL LIGHT
LOVE ME TENDER AND TREAT ME RIGHT

V2
LONELY BOY GOT THE G.I. BLUES
THAT'S ALL RIGHT MAMA'S WATCHING OVER YOU
WISE MEN SAY IF YOU DON'T BE CRUEL
YOU'LL GET TO HEAVEN WEARING BLUE SUEDE SHOES

CHORUS
SINGING WITH ANGELS, SAFE IN GOD'S PROMISED LAND
SINGING WITH ANGELS, WALKING HAND IN HAND
SINGING WITH ANGELS, IT'S PART OF GOD'S MASTER PLAN
THERE'S SO MANY ANGELS, WALKING HAND IN HAND
WHAT A BEAUTIFUL BAND

V3
I GOT A WOMAN SHE'S MY HAPPINESS
DON'T LEAVE ME NOW, IN MY LONELINESS
HEARTBREAK HOTEL, I WAS COUNTING ON YOU
THOUGHT I HAD A LOT OF LIVING TO DO
THE BLUE MOON OF KENTUCKY SHINES
BURNING LOVE MAKES SUSPICIOUS MINDS
MYSTERY TRAIN HEADING FOR THE LIGHT
GRACELANDS STAR, BURNING BRIGHT

REPEAT CHORUS

(talk)
Elvis has left the building.

Featured on In the Spotlight 2011, Cherry Red Records

Andy Scott, Steve Grant and myself got together to
make the album Back to the Drive. Mike Chapman
was executive producer and wrote the title track. They
both came over to my house and we revisited the aborted
album from a few months before, picking the best songs
to re-record. This one, though, is one that was written
new for this project. It all started with a comment I
made. I have a history and habit or talking poetically
and in titles... it's happened all my life... and so... let me
say it now

I don't do gentle. This is a song that has been live on
my stage since it was written. It works.

I DON'T DO GENTLE

(S. Quatro/Andy Scott/S. Grant) Butterfly/Rak/ Fanfare Musik Verlag

V1
WHY AM I ALWAYS SITTING ALONE ON A SATURDAY NIGHT
WHY DOES EVERYBODY THINK I'M ALWAYS GETTING READY TO FIGHT
WELL IF YOU WANT TO GET CLOSE TO ME
YOU GOTTA OPEN UP YOUR EYES AND SEE
THAT I GOT A GOOD HEART
BUT I'M A LITTLE MIS-UNDERSTOOD

CHORUS
WELL I DON'T DO GENTLE
I AIN'T SENTIMENTAL
NO I DON'T DO GENTLE,
BUT I'M PRETTY GOOD COMPANY

V2
WHY AM I SITTING HERE BY THE PHONE WAITING FOR YOU TO CALL
WELL I'M TELLING YOU SOMETHING HONEY
KIND OF FUNNY THAT YOU BOTHERED AT ALL
I KNOW I AIN'T SUGAR AND SPICE
BUT YOU STILL GOTTA TREAT ME NICE
IF YOU WANNA LOVE ME TENDER
THEN YOU REALLY GOT TO TREAT ME RIGHT

REPEAT CHORUS

Featured on Back to the Drive 2006

And, from the same album, another comment I made...
I remember being on the phone, can't remember who to
though, damn... would like to thank them... I said,

'I was born making noise.' While we were laying down
tracks at Andy's home studio, as per normal we gathered
around the kitchen hub with a glass of red to relax.
I happened to mention this title... and it immediately led to a
song. I now use this as an intro and outro... Andy providing
the vocal... 'Ladies and gentleman, please welcome to the stage,
all the way from Detroit City, U.S.A... the queen of rock
and roll...'

• long may it all continue

BORN MAKING NOISE

(S. Quatro, A. Scott, S. Grant) Butterfly/Rak/ Fanfare Musik Verlag

V1
I GOT THE TOUGHEST LITTLE ACT IN THIS GODDAMN TOWN
I GOT THE MEANEST LITTLE MOUTH FOR MILES AROUND
MAKE NO MISTAKE ABOUT IT, I AIN'T NO SHRINKING VIOLET
NO NEED TO CONTEMPLATE IT, JUST DON'T YOU UNDERRATE IT
YOU CAN'T INTIMIDATE IT, THIS LITTLE LADY LOVES LIFE

CHORUS
I WAS BORN MAKING NOISE
I MAY BE A GIRL BUT I'M ONE OF THE BOYS
I WAS BORN MAKING NOISE
AIN'T NOBODY GONNA PUT ME DOWN

V2
I GOT THE SWEETEST LITTLE SMILE IN THIS NEIGHBOURHOOD
KILLER EYES THAT VAPORISE, I'M BAD WHEN I'M GOOD
DON'T YOU DEBATE ABOUT, YOU WANT IT I GOT IT
NO NEED TO CRITICISE IT, NO NEED TO ANALYSE IT
BUT YOU CAN FANTASISE IT, THIS LEATHER LADY LOVES LIFE

CHORUS

V3
WELL I'M THE TOUGHEST LITTLE CHICK DON'T YOU MAKE ME
MAD
I GOT THE MEANEST LITTLE MOUTH, I'M GOOD WHEN I'M BAD
MAKE NO MISTAKE ABOUT IT, I AIN'T NO SHRINKING VIOLET
DON'T TRY TO KEEP ME QUIET, I'M LOUD I CAN'T DENY IT
IT'S TIME TO START A RIOT, THIS LEATHER LADY LOVES LIFE

CHORUS

Featured on Back to the Drive 2006

Again recording the Back to the Drive album, and again, I had the title and quite a bit of the lyrics, and again, after a session we gathered around the kitchen hub at Andy's home studio, and again, drinking one of my favourite Australian red wines, Jaspers Hill, Emily's Paddock... irresistible.

The idea of this one is what has happened to the industry today, just my humble opinion. In my day, you got into music because you couldn't not be in the music. It wasn't a job, it was, and is, a calling. With the way things have gone today, it is much more a case of people getting in the business to 'be famous'... hence the Andy Warhol line.

This too has been on and off in the live show depending where I am performing. I tend to always do it in Australia... I don't know why, perhaps it's Jasper Hill's fault!!

15 MINUTES OF FAME

(S. Quatro/Andy Scott/S. Grant) Butterfly/Rak/ Fanfare Musik Verlag

V1
EGOS COME AND EGOS GO
ON THE STAIRWAY TO SUCCESS
JUSTIFYING OUR EXISTENCE
PUTTING US TO THE TEST
WE CAN ALL FALL DOWN THE MIGHTY AND TALL
WE CAN ALL LOSE OUR CROWN
AND THE ONES YOU HURT ON THE ROCKY ROAD UP
TRIP YOU UP ON THE WAY BACK DOWN.

CHORUS
15 MINUTES OF FAME ANDY WARHOL USED TO SAY
15 MINUTES OF FAME THEN THEY STEAL YOUR STAR AWAY
COME ON PLAY THE GAME COME SHINE A LIGHT DOWN ON ME
TAKE A BOW, THIS IS NOW, 15… 15 MINUTES OF FAME

V2
MONEY MAKES THE WORLD GO ROUND
OUR LOSS BECOMES THEIR GAIN
SELFISH FINGERS GRAB IT ALL
GREED IS THEIR DOMAIN,
WE CAN ALL WANT MORE BUT DIAMONDS AND PEARLS
ARE THE NEEDS OF A LONELY SOUL
AND THE DREAMS YOU DREAM IN YOUR DARKEST HOUR
ARE DESIRES IN CONTROL

CHORUS

BRIDGE
15 MINUTES IS ALL YOU GET, MONEY AND FAME GONNA GET YOU YET
15 MINUTES IS ALL YOU GET, SO GET IT WHILE YOU CAN
15 MINUTES IS ALL YOU GET, MONEY AND FAME AND NO REGRET
15 MINUTES IS ALL YOU GET SO GET IT WHILE YOU CAN

CHORUS

Featured on Back to the Drive 2006

Mike Chapman and I recording our first complete album together for over 30 years... We had always worked on various things but not a whole album. It was interesting to do this, meeting up again with everything we had gathered along the way both in life, and musically. I have had a good friend in Australia for many years... he knows who he is so I do not have to 'name' him, which I feel would embarrass him. I wrote this song for him, and about him... he has kept me sane on many many long tours. One of life's good people. Happy to have him in my life.

• my mother on my shoulder

HURT WITH YOU

(S. Quatro) Butterfly/Rak

V1
SO LAY YOUR WEAPONS ON THE GROUND
I'LL TIP TOE IN WITHOUT A SOUND
YOU KNOW I COULD BREAK YOU IF I TRIED
BUT I WON'T TRY.. I JUST WANT TO TELL YOU THAT

V2
NEED TO KNOCK THESE FENCES DOWN
SO I CAN TURN YOUR HEART AROUND
YOU KNOW I CAN SEE WHAT'S TRAPPED INSIDE
I WON'T LET IT DIE, .. I DON'T MEAN TO MAKE YOU CRY BUT

CHORUS
I NEED TO HURT WITH YOU, I NEED TO HURT WITH YOU
SOMETIMES IT MAY SEEM CRUEL
WHAT CAN I DO, WHAT CAN I DO
I NEED TO HURT WITH YOU

V3
SO TAKE THAT PICTURE OFF THE WALL
BREAK THE GLASS, THEN LET IT FALL
MEMORIES OF SOMEONE YOU ONCE KNEW,
WON'T GET YOU THROUGH
LIFE IS LETHAL, WE SURVIVE IT

REPEAT CHORUS

BRIDGE
BEEN THINKING ABOUT IT… BEEN RUNNING IT 'ROUND MY BRAIN
YOU CAN LIVE WITHOUT IT, .. TIME TO LET GO OF YOUR PAIN

REPEAT CHORUS

Featured on In The Spotlight 2011

This song was written maybe 10 years ago. It is a song that happens once in a lifetime, and you don't even see it coming. I have always referred to it as my 'masterpiece'. I still have the original demo with me going from piano to guitar and back again. I doubt if I will ever write a song like this again.

When we were doing the Quatro, Scott and Powell album, I sent Andy and Don the demo, expecting them to say, oh no Suzi, this is not suitable for this album... but they said just the opposite. They loved it. Wow... that was a surprise. It is a beautiful rendition.

My idea was to take you through all the phases love goes through from beginning to end.

I am very proud of this song.

BROKEN PIECES SUITE

(S.Quatro) Butterfly/Rak

Refrain
BROKEN PIECES, BROKEN PIECES, BROKEN PIECES, BROKEN PIECES

PART 1
DRIFT UP SLOWLY TO THE LIGHT, TOUCH THE STARS ABOVE
WHISPER SOFTLY TO THE NIGHT, ALL YOU'RE THINKING OF
(REPEAT) WE HAD A DREAM IT WAS SURREAL
WE MADE OUR PLANS, LIFE WAS IDEAL
AND SO WE SAILED INTO THE SUN
NOW THERE'S NOWHERE LEFT TO RUN
FLY ON WINGS OF, A SILVER DOVE
BROKEN PIECES OF LOVE, BROKEN PIECES OF LOVE

Repeat refrain

PART 2
FOREVER I WALK THIS PATH ALONE
HOPING TO FIND THAT PLACE UNKNOWN
CAN'T EXPLAIN THE WAY I FEEL
BUT IT'S MY HEART THAT CANNOT HEAL
EVERY STEP I TAKE IS ONE MORE STEP TO FALL
FOREVER I LOOK FOR SOMETHING MORE
BUT I DON'T KNOW WHAT I'M SEARCHING FOR
IF IT'S LOVE ETERNAL FLAME
WHY IS LOVE A LOSING GAME
BEHIND EVERY DOOR IS ONE MORE EMPTY HALL

Repeat refrain

PART 3
TRUTH WILL ALWAYS SOMEHOW FIND A WAY
TRUTH WILL ALWAYS STAND UP STRAIGHT AND TALL
THOSE PRETTY LIES YOU WEAVE YOU WEAR THEM WELL
THEY'LL TRIP YOU UP, YOU'LL STUMBLE THEN YOU'LL FALL
THERE'S NO MISTAKEN, IT'S A CHANCE I'M TAKING ON YOU, ON YOU
WILL I BE FORSAKEN, IF I DANCE THIS DANCE WITH YOU
WITH YOU WITH YOU

REPEAT PART 1

WE HAD A DREAM IT WAS SURREAL,
WE MADE OUR PLANS, LIFE WAS IDEAL
AND SO WE SAILED INTO THE SUN
NOW THERE'S NOWHERE LEFT TO RUN
FLY ON WINGS OF, A SILVER DOVE
BROKEN PIECES OF LOVE, BROKEN PIECES OF LOVE
Repeat refrain

Featured on Quatro, Scott and Powell, 2017

Quatro, Scott and Powell, or QSP, which consisted of myself, Andy Scott, original lead guitarist of Sweet, and Don Powell, original drummer of Slade, came into being because my husband had the idea years and years ago. We never had the time, for a long time, and then, hooray, it was the time! It was 2016 and finally, in 2017, this album was released. We first went in with covers, 2 choices each, including my husband, to help us to 'find' the direction of the three of us together. Hubby, Rainer Haas, is very proud, and rightly so, that the group was his idea and that one of his two choices ended up being the opening track on the album.

Once we got into the swing of things, I came up with the title, and started to write on guitar 'Long Way From Home'. I showed Andy what I had at the next session, and I explained that it is exactly the kind of life we have all lived. He then came up with the excellent middle addition which I have called the chorus... although strictly speaking there is no verse and no chorus... it all rolls into one... just like being on the road... and finally, the both of us made the whole song take shape. I do love this one. And I am proud and happy to have worked with these two fine musicians, who I am lucky enough to call friends.

PS. the album charted at number 16 in Australia, while QSP were the opening act for my Suzi Quatro tour... confusing... you bet... but... not for a Gemini!!! (tongue firmly in cheek)

• Detroit gig, circa 1968

122

LONG WAY FROM HOME

(S.Quatro/A .Scott) Butterfly/Rak/Fanfare Musik Verlag

V1
A DIRTY NEON SIGN, DOWN A DUSTY ROAD
RIDING THE CAFFEINE HIGH, ANOTHER MIDNIGHT LOW
YES WE'RE A LONG WAY FROM HOME
GYPSIES RIDE THAT WIND, WHEREVER IT MAY BLOW
BITTERSWEET DREAMS BACK WHEN, THE ONLY LIFE WE KNOW
YES WE'RE A LONG WAY FROM HOME
YES WE'RE A LONG LONG WAY, FROM HOME

WILL WE EVER FIND OUR WAY BACK HOME
WILL WE EVER FIND OUR WAY BACK HOME

V2
WE DANCE A LONG WHITE LINE,
GOD KNOWS WHAT'S ROUND THE BEND
MOONLIGHT UP OUR MINDS,
BEGINNING WHERE WE END
YES WE'RE A LONG WAY FROM HOME
YES WE'RE A LONG LONG WAY

CHORUS
BLINDED BY THE LIGHTS (BLINDED BY THE LIGHTS)
DRIVING THROUGH THE ENDLESS NIGHT (THROUGH THE
ENDLESS NIGHT)
OH OH WE'RE A LONG WAY FROM HOME (LONG WAY FROM HOME)
OH OH STILL A LONG WAY FROM HOME
(WE'RE A LONG WAY FROM HOME)
HOME (SUCH A LONG WAY FROM HOME)
HOME (IT'S A LONG WAY FROM HOME)
OH OH A LONG WAY FROM HOME (OH A LONG WAY FROM HOME)
OH OH STILL A LONG WAY FROM HOME

V3
A DIRTY NEON SIGN, DOWN A DUSTY ROAD
RIDING THAT CAFFEINE HIGH, ANOTHER MIDNIGHT LOW

LONG WAY FROM HOME, LONG WAY FROM HOME
YES WE'RE A (LONG LONG WAY FROM HOME, LONG LONG WAY
FROM HOME)
WE'RE A LONG WAY FROM HOME
(LONG LONG WAY FROM HOME X 2)
YEAH, A LONG WAY FROM HOME

Featured on Quatro, Scott and Powell, 2017

For me, and I said so onstage on our Australia tour, this next song became the 'heart' of the sessions. I had an idea... and it really came flying out, on guitar again, which I admittedly don't play very well, but good enough to write on. The first verse and basic chorus was in place so I phoned Andy... It was 8:30 a.m... and he was on tour!! Timing is everything folks.

He phoned about a week later and said, 'Okay, I cannot get that song out of my mind'... so when he got back, I took a trip to his place, and we finished the song. It is a beauty. And again, I remember being around the kitchen hub... of course with Jasper's Hill in our wine glasses, with Andy, his wife Jane and myself, listening to our rough demo... and we were all three crying. That's when you know you have something special.

There are two versions of this on the album, because nobody could choose between them. The band version, and the orchestra version created by Mike Batt. I LOVED singing this song on stage... goose bumps every time.

PAIN

(S. Quatro/A. Scott) Butterfly/Rak/Fanfare Musik Verlag

V1
NEVER A DAY, NEVER A DAY GOES BY
NOTHING TO SAY, NO-ONE TO ASK ME WHY
AND I, I CAN'T STAND THE PAIN
IT'S COMING ROUND AGAIN
AND IT'S BRINGING ME DOWN

CHORUS
WE ALL GOTTA FEEL PAIN SOMETIMES
WE ALL GOTTA GO THERE ONE TIME
WE ALL GOTTA WALK THAT FINE LINE
IF YOU OPEN YOUR HEART
YOU'RE GONNA CRY CRY CRY
LOVE RIPS YOU APART, YOU'RE GONNA CRY CRY CRY CRY
AND FEEL THE PAIN

V2
HEARD SOMEONE SAY, SOMEBODY SAID THOSE WORDS
I SAY THOSE WORDS, BUT NOW THEY JUST SOUND ABSURD
AND I, I CAN'T PLAY THIS GAME
IT'S DRIVING ME INSANE
AND IT'S BRINGING ME DOWN

REPEAT CHORUS

AND FEEL THE PAIN, AND FEEL THE PAIN
CRY CRY CRY CRY CRY
AND FEEL THE PAIN

Featured on Quatro, Scott and Powell, 2017

While making In the Spotlight with Mike Chapman, I met
and worked with Nat Allison, a fabulous musician and
singer... and, more important, a nice person. We have become
good friends over the years, she has stayed at my house, we
have written some songs together, not released yet, and she has
graced my stage in Australia several times now, which I hope
will continue until this sweet little rock 'n' roller stops. I have
included a couple of our co-compositions. She is a true talent
and I just love her. In fact, my nickname for her is 'my girl'.
(Well I am from Detroit!)

• before gig, waiting, waiting , waiting...
  Australia, red hot summer tour.

KILLING TIME

(S. Quatro/N. Allison) Butterfly/Rak

V1
I DIDN'T WANNA NEED YOU, FOR THE LONGEST TIME
I DIDN'T WANNA TOUCH YOU, OR TO CALL YOU MINE
I NEVER WANTED NOTHING I COULD NOT DEFINE
NOW WE'RE OUTTA TIME, OUTTA TIME

CHORUS
WHAT'S THE POINT OF ACHING ONCE YOU KNOW IT'S TRUE
YOU'RE ONLY KILLING TIME UNTIL IT'S KILLING YOU
WHAT'S THE POINT OF CRYING WHEN I ALWAYS KNEW
YOU WERE ONLY KILLING TIME KILLING TIME, KILLING TIME
ONLY KILLING TIME KILLING TIME KILLING TIME

V2
NOW ALL I DO IS NEED YOU, IT'S BEEN THE LONGEST TIME
AND I ONLY WANNA TOUCH YOU, AND TO CALL YOU MINE
NOW ALL I HAVE IS SOMETHING, THAT WE CAN'T DEFINE
AND WE'RE OUTTA TIME, OUTTA TIME

CHORUS

BRIDGE
I WAS YOUR SECRET
YOU WERE MY WEAKNESS
LONELY HEART, I WAS DEFENCELESS

REPEAT CHORUS

YOU WERE ONLY KILLING TIME KILLING TIME KILLING TIME X 3

Currently unreleased

And the second Quatro/Allison song to be included. Of the two this is my favourite, and I really think it suits Nat's voice. She does a beautiful job on it.

Interesting arrangement too, which is amazing because it was not easy putting these tracks down. The studio I had booked was not suitable to our needs and we really struggled to create anything, but in the end, us 'pro's pulled it all together. I think we did 5 tracks altogether.

Myself on bass, lead vox, and backing vox, Jez Davies on keys, Tim Reyland on percussion, Nat on guitar, lead vox, and backing vox.

And to quote a genuine genius, 'If music be the food of love, play on.'

MILLION MILES

(S. Quatro/N. Allison) Butterfly/Rak

V1
WHEN THE TRUTH BEGINS TO FALL
AND YOU LIE, INSIDE YOU WALL
AS THE PAGES OF MY LIFE BEGIN TO TURN
I KNOW I'M GONNA GET BURNED
WHO CAN SAY WHO'S WRONG OR RIGHT
YOU'RE BOTH HUNGRY FOR THE FIGHT
AND THE REASON FOR YOUR LOVE JUST DISAPPEARS
I GOTTA GET OUTTA HERE.

CHORUS
A MILLION MILES, A MILLION SMILES
ALL OF THE TEARS, FEEDING OUR FEARS, PAYING THE PRICE
A MILLION MILES, A MILLION SMILES
NO-ONE'S TO BLAME WE'RE JUST PLAYING THE GAME
IT'S A ROLL OF THE DICE
SO BEFORE YOU SAY FOREVER, YOU BETTER THINK TWICE
YOU BETTER THINK TWICE

V2
WHEN THREE WORDS BEGIN TO FADE
CUZ THERE'S NOTHING LEFT TO SAY
ALL THOSE MEMORIES OF LOVE HAVE DISAPPEARED
I GOTTA GET OUTTA HERE

REPEAT CHORUS

SO BEFORE YOU SAY FOREVER, BEFORE YOU SAY FOREVER

BRIDGE
NEVER THOUGHT I'D LEAVE YOU, THOUGHT I COULD BELIEVE YOU
NOW WE'RE STANDING ON THE EDGE
OF THOSE PROMISES WE SAID
THIS REALITY, WE CAN'T DENY

REPEAT CHORUS

YOU BETTER THINK TWICE X 4
NEVER SO TOGETHER, OR SO FAR APART

Not released yet, only on demo

129

And now... if not my best album, certainly one of my best albums ever. It came completely unexpectedly. My son wanted to write with me for a long time, and it just never felt right. Then one day he said to me... 'Mum, I need to write with you.' That to me translated as... he was ready. Long story short, we first did a few demos when all of a sudden we all realised, myself, Richard, my son, and Mike Curtis who owns and engineers his studio (who I just love by the way), that it was serious and we were making an album. Five minutes later we had a record deal. All by accident... which is how the truly wonderful things happen in life.

This first one that I have chosen from the album No Control is something that came from a guitar lick that I had been doing for years and years. What a relief to finally make a song out of it. It is my nudge nudge wink wink to reality talent shows... which I first visited in '15 Minutes of Fame'... and all these years later, I still feel the same. And... I won't lie that I don't watch them... they are, of course, very entertaining... that is a no brainer... we are now, in lockdown, writing for the next album, 12 songs completed. Hopefully when this lyric book is released... lockdown will be a distant memory.

• A couple of my babies.

EASY PICKIN'S

(S. Quatro/R. Tuckey) Butterfly/Rak

V1
CHEAP CALL, DREAMING IS EASY
BIG BOSS, THREW THE TALENT AWAY
GLASS HOUSE, WILL HIDE YOU NOTHING
SUN DRIED, THEN YOU'RE OUT IN THE RAIN

V2
STAND TALL, BRIGHT LIGHTS SHINING
APPLAUSE, ON THE EDGE OF A WAVE
QUICK FALL, GOT A BAD MOON RISING
LOST CAUSE, THAT NOBODY CAN SAVE

CHORUS
EASY PICKIN'S IT'S NOWHERE YOU WANNA BE
EASY PICKIN'S YOU'RE SELLING YOUR SOUL FOR FREE
YOU AIN'T NO LOSER, SO DON'T TAKE NO CHARITY
EASY PICKIN'S IS NOWHERE THAT YOU WANT TO BE

V3
HIGH RISE REACH FOR THE BRASS RING
HOLD ON, TILL THE MUSIC DIES
LISTEN CLOSE, THAT'S REALITY SINGING
LOW DOWN, WHERE MEDIOCRITY LIES

REPEAT CHORUS

Featured on No Control, 2019

My son arrived one sunny afternoon - song writing session, out on the patio... beautiful summer luckily... and unusual for England, played me this sequence... and I said, 'Inside - we need to go electric.' We both went to the front room, plugged in, and I immediately started to play 'lead' bass, which is very very unlike me... I started playing melody lines... I said to Richard, 'This song is called Bass Line'... and it was.

Doing the lyrics I was able to delve into what the bass line actually was other than the obvious. It's a very interesting concept, both musically and lyrically, and... and... and... I PLAYED THE SOLO ON IT ON THE BASS!!! Yea!!

THE BASS LINE

(S. Quatro/R. Tuckey) Butterfly/Rak

V1
YOU GOTTA LONG WAY TO GO
SO WHY YOU WANNA MOVE SO SLOW
IT'S IN THE POCKET DEEP AND LOW
SO SOCK IT TO ME LET IT FLOW

CHORUS
BASS LINE, FOLLOW THAT BASS LINE
STRAIGHT DOWN THE FRET LINE
FOLLOW THAT BASS LINE
WALKING DOWN THE BASS LINE WON'T LEAD YOU ASTRAY

V2
PLAY IT SWEET THE WAY YOU FEEL
PLAY IT TILL YOU KNOW IT'S REAL
KEEP IT CLOSE AND DRIVE IT HOME
TAKE IT BACK WHERE YOU BELONG

REPEAT CHORUS

WALKING DOWN THAT BASS LINE WON'T LEAD YOU ASTRAY
WALKING DOWN THAT BASS LINE, WILL SHOW YOU THE WAY

Featured on No Control, 2019

This song is the first song my son and I ever wrote together. He played this riff, I liked it and I remember saying... 'Yes, I can do something with this.' I had a couple of other things to do so we booked up the studio Richard recommended, CDS, owned and operated by Mike Curtis who also did the engineering, and there a great creative team, and friendship, was formed. What a joy working here, for me, my son, and all the musicians who took part. Lyric wise, it seems to be a very natural path... you let somebody in... then the 'jerk' appears and I don't mean 'me'. This song did go through a change from when we demo'd it to when we recorded it, lyrically and vocally. It's cool.

• Attitude.. thats all, just Attitude.

DON'T DO ME WRONG

(S. Quatro/R. Tuckey) Butterfly/Rak

V1
I'M SPEAKING MY MIND, MY ARROW'S IN FLIGHT
IT MAY BE UNKIND BUT, YOU'RE GONNA HEAR ME TONIGHT
IT'S TIME FOR A SHOWDOWN, IT'S TIME TO COME CLEAN
I'M GIVING YOU THE PART OF ME, THAT YOU'VE NEVER SEEN

I DON'T WANT TO NEED NOBODY
I DON'T WANT TO WANT NOBODY
ALL I WANT IS TO BE SOMEBODY

CHORUS
DON'T DO ME WRONG.. DON'T DO ME WRONG,
DON'T DO ME WRONG.. DON'T YOU DO ME WRONG

V2
I GAVE YOU THE KEY TO MY INSIDE TRACK
YOU GAVE ME RED ROSES, YOU ALWAYS PAINTED THEM BLACK
I CAN'T KEEP ON WALKING ON BROKEN GLASS
I CAN'T KEEP ON ACTING THAT, YOU'RE NOT A PAIN IN THE ASS
(CUZ YOU ARE BABY)

I DON'T WANT TO NEED NOBODY
I DON'T WANT TO WANT NOBODY
ALL I WANT IS TO BE SOMEBODY

DON'T DO ME WRONG, DON'T DO ME WRONG, DON'T DO ME
WRONG.. NO NO NO DON'T YOU DO ME WRONG.

REPEAT CHORUS AND FADE

Featured on No Control, 2019

And another song that started with a riff from Richard. This immediately suggested a title which immediately suggested a lyric.

I twisted it though, if you notice, I'm saying, I'm going home, but I don't mean to a physical home... I mean home to ME... home where I belong. The most lonely you can be is when your are with someone, and still feel alone... in this case it is better to be alone. Lesson learned... and if not... learn it... a word of advice... Been there, cried the tears, felt the heartbreak... whoops, another lyric.

GOING HOME

(S. Quatro/R. Tuckey) Butterfly/Rak

V1
YOU CRAWLED INSIDE OF MY HEAD
AND THEN YOU CRAWLED IN MY BED
I DIDN'T THINK YOU WOULD HURT ME
AND WHEN I TURN OUT THE LIGHT
I KNOW THAT SOMETHING AIN'T RIGHT
CUZ EVERY NIGHT YOU DESERT ME

V2
HOW CAN YOU LAY BY MY SIDE
YOU ALWAYS WITHDRAW AND HIDE
DON'T YOU KNOW HOW I'M FEELING
GOT A DECISION TO MAKE
BEFORE MY MIND DOES A BREAK
AND SO I STARE AT THE CEILING

CHORUS
GOING HOME, HOME ALONE, GOING HOME, HOME ALONE
FLYING FREE, I'M A ROLLING STONE
GOING HOME WHERE I BELONG

V3
YOU RIPPED A HOLE IN MY HEART
AND THEN YOU RIPPED ME APART
UNTIL OUR LOVE HAD NO MEANING
AND NOW I'VE MADE UP MY MIND
TO LEAVE THIS HEARTACHE BEHIND
I'M ON MY WAY TO THE HEALING

REPEAT CHORUS

REPEAT FIRST VERSE

REPEAT CHORUS AND FADE

Featured on No Control, 2019

Closing track on No Control. This was my blues with a difference. Had the riff, had the title, in fact the whole song could not wait. I was on the road, so finished this one on my own. It's a true story, whose origin will remain locked in my heart. I am going to take the writer's 5th on this, on the grounds that it might incriminate me.

Vote for me and I'll set you free'... yeah... right!

• a soundcheck, some stage, somewhere, some year.

GOING DOWN BLUES

(S. Quatro) Butterfly/Rak

V1
WHAT WAS YA THINKING WHEN YOU WROTE YOUR BOOK
WHO WAS YA SCREWING TO TAKE WHO YOU TOOK
HOW COULD YOU SEE ME WHEN YOU NEVER LOOKED
MUST A BEEN FISHING NOW YOU'RE ON THE HOOK

CHORUS
YOU GOT THE GOING DOWN BLUES,
YOU GOT THE GOING DOWN BLUES.

V2
KARMA WILL GET YA EACH WAY THAT YA TURN
KARMA WILL TEACH YOU THINGS YOU NEVER LEARNED
JUMP IN YOUR FIRE, GET READY TO BURN
FED YOUR DESIRE, NOW EAT WHAT YOU'VE EARNED

CHORUS
YOU GOT THE GOING DOWN BLUES
YOU GOT THE GOING DOWN BLUES
SO PAY THAT GOING ROUND DUES
YOU GOT THE GOING DOWN BLUES

BRIDGE
LOVE IS A TREASON YOU'D DIE FOR
NOW I'M WALKING, I'M WALKING, I'M WALKING AWAY
AND CLOSING THAT DOOR
YOU GAVE ME NO REASON TO STAY FOR
AIN'T GONNA TAKE IT NO MORE, NO MORE, NO MORE

V3
WHY THIS OBSESSION TO BREAK ME IN TWO
WHAT THE HELL WRONG DID I DO TO YOU
IF MY CONFESSIONS THE METHOD YOU CHOOSE
PUSH THE KNIFE DEEPER IT'S SURE TO CUT YOU

REPEAT CHORUS.

Featured on No Control, 2019

And another riff... Richard is good on riffs... and I am good on developing said riffs.

This was one he nearly didn't show me because he thought it was too heavy!! I was immediately interested. It says quite a statement. This is a heavy duty world, and we all have to work hard to survive in it. The person in this story is somebody who does just that... survives with no conscience whatsoever... no judgement... maybe he's right, maybe he's wrong?

Maybe it really is survival of the fittest.

HEAVY DUTY

(S. Quatro/R. Tuckey) Butterfly/Rak

CHORUS
TO CARRY THAT WEIGHT YOU GOTTA STAND UP STRAIGHT
IT'S A HEAVY DUTY WORLD HEAVY DUTY WORLD
TO CARRY THAT LOAD YOU GOTTA GRAB ON AND HOLD
IT'S A HEAVY DUTY WORLD, HEAVY DUTY WORLD
HEAVY DUTY WORLD….
HEAVY DUTY

V1
IT YOU GOTTA FIGHT IT, I KNOW YOU KINDA LIKE IT
AND YOU TAKE NO BLAME
BABY WHEN YOU USE IT, CHOOSE IT AND ABUSE IT
WELL YOU GOT NO SHAME
EVERYBODY WANTS WHAT EVERYBODY HAS
BUT YOU DON'T PLAY THAT WAY

REPEAT CHORUS

V2
TALK ABOUT SURVIVING, DUCKING AND A DIVING
WELL THAT'S YOUR WAY
GIVE A HIGH FIVING, JUMPING AND A JIVING
JUST ANOTHER DAY
TAKE NO PRISONER LEAVE NO WITNESSES
THAT'S HOW YOU MAKE IT THROUGH THE DAY

REPEAT CHORUS

Featured on No Control, 2019

Strings... in my opinion, one of my top compositions of all time. Not only a great tune, but the message is so so important, especially to what we have currently gone through. I hope it is appropriate to say 'gone' through by the time this book is published!! At the end of the day, we are all one species, one people... and are all held together by... STRINGS. The recording of this is superb... all musicians played a part, Jez Davis on keys, Tim Reyland on percussion, Richard Tuckey on guitar, me on bass, Toby Guckelhorn on sax, Dick Hanson on trumpet, Ray Beavis on sax and responsible for the outstanding horn arrangement, Lousie Hartley and Dionne Moss on backing vocals... damn... what a track!! (and of course Mike Curtis in his chair, permanently in front of the console, wonder if he has moved yet?)

• backstage, some stage, somewhere, some year

STRINGS

(S. Quatro/R. Tuckey)

V1
EVERYBODY TRIES TO SLIDE DOWN SLOWLY
EVERYBODY TRIES TO PAVE THEIR OWN WAY
TAKE IT SLOWLY TO THAT SPACE CALLED SADNESS
MAKE IT LONELY, TO THE END OF THE DAY

V2
EVERYBODY HITS THE HIGHWAY RUNNING
FLYING HERE AND THERE AND GOD KNOWS WHERE
NEVER THINKING 'BOUT THAT TRAIN THAT'S RUNNING
ANOTHER PASSENGER, JUST ROLLING AWAY

CHORUS
STRINGS, THEY HOLD US ALL FOREVER
STRINGS, THEY'RE ALL THOSE SONGS WE SING
STRINGS, THEY JOIN US ALL TOGETHER
STRINGS, STRINGS STRINGS

V3
WE COME INTO THIS WORLD WITH BOTH EYES OPEN
THEN WE LEAVE THIS WORLD WITH BOTH EYES CLOSED
IN THE MIDDLE OF THIS PLACE CALLED MADNESS
HIDING SECRETS DEEP WHERE NOBODY GOES.

STRINGS, STRINGS, STRINGS, STRINGS, STRINGS STRINGS

REPEAT CHORUS

Featured on No Control, 2019

I have been asked so many times... which self-penned song best describes me... finally after writing this one with my son Richard, (great guitar riff)... Here is the answer. This song is me 100 % ME... it is how I feel, it is my thrust, it is how I have survived both in the world and in this business. I even recite the chorus onstage just to make sure the audience gets it. Do you?

First single release from album, great video.

NO SOUL / NO CONTROL

(S. Quatro/R. Tuckey) Butterfly/Rak

V1
IF YOU THINK I'M WRONG, IF YOU THINK I'M RIGHT
GOTTA PLAY IT STRONG GOTTA PUT UP A FIGHT
KEEP IT CLOSE TO HAND, TILL YOU UNDERSTAND
YOU CAN'T TAKE THE BIGGEST PART IT'S NOT IN MY PLAN

I GOTTA HOLD ON TO ME
I GOTTA HOLD ON TO ME
SAVE ME SAVE ME SAVE ME SAVE ME
I GOTTA HOLD ONTO ME

CHORUS
YOU CAN'T TAKE AWAY MY SOUL
YOU CAN'T BREAK ME CUZ I'M IN CONTROL
YOU CAN'T TAKE MY HEART MY MIND THIS TIME I WON'T LET GO
YOU CAN'T TAKE AWAY MY SOUL NO NO NO NO.. NO NO NO

V2
FALL INTO YOUR MIRE, TRAPPED IN HOT DESIRE
I CAN'T PLAY IT COOL WHEN MY BODY'S ON FIRE
IF THE LIE IS TRUE, I'LL TURN IT BACK ON YOU
STAND UP AND BE COUNTED , YEA THAT'S ALL I CAN DO

I GOTTA HOLD ON TO ME (DO YA GET IT)
I GOTTA HOLD, HOLD ON TIGHT TO ME

REPEAT CHORUS

Featured on No Control, 2019

This song means so much to me that when I do this live, at the end of my show, believe it or not... you can hear a pin drop... I shed a tear every time.

Again, it is a true story, which I will keep to myself, and leave the reader/listener to create his/her own scenario. All I will say in explanation is... we can waste a lot of emotion (although emotion is never truly wasted!!)... and energy trying to make things okay with our loved ones, explaining, arguing, retreating, attacking, coercing, plotting, planning, and all for nothing... because in the end there is only one reality... it is MY HEART... ON THE LINE (always was, always will be)... it's in my artistic DNA.

• Vive le Rock awards, changed the lettering on statue for digital release, perfect picture.

HEART ON THE LINE

(S. Quatro) Butterfly/Rak

V1
YOU DON'T KNOW WHAT YOU PUT ME THROUGH
IT'S BEEN HELL TRYING TO TALK TO YOU
LIES ARE WEAK, SO IT'S TRUTH I'LL SPEAK
UNDER YOUR SPELL, I'VE BEEN AN EMPTY SHELL

CHORUS
AND IT WAS MY HEART ON THE LINE
IT WAS MY HEART, ALL THE TIME
ALL THOSE DREAMS I THOUGHT WERE MINE
MILES AWAY, MILES AWAY
AND IT WAS MY HEART ON THE LINE
IT WAS MY HEART ALL THE TIME
LIKE A POEM THAT'S LOST ITS RHYME
MILES AWAY, MILES AWAY, MILES AWAY

V2
WHO CAN SAY, WHO PLAYS THE FOOL
LOVE'S A GAME, BUT WHO MAKES THE RULES
I WAS BLIND TOO BLIND TO SEE
I GAVE YOU EVERYTHING YOU DENIED TO ME

REPEAT CHORUS

Featured on No Control, 2019

This song has a story that goes along with it. We had returned, Shirlie, myself and daughter Laura, from the studio; both Laura and Shirlie had been doing some backing vocals. We got home, Laura went up to bed – I believe she was pregnant with Amy at the time – and Shirlie and I opened up a bottle of good red and started to talk.

We spoke, for some reason, about relationships, and I ventured into mine with my daughter, which I am sure she will agree has not always been easy, we are too much alike and have the exact same triggers, which we have dissected many times through the years. Anyway, I made a comment, as is my way, to Shirlie, 'Doesn't she know I would walk through the fire for her?'... OMG... EUREKA... a song... we grabbed the guitar and took paper and pen out to the patio.

Wait a minute Shirlie... I went up and woke Laura... 'You must write this song with us, it's important.' So she got out of bed, came downstairs in her pyjamas and we wrote this song. It became a duet between mother and daughter... just as it should be.

I'LL WALK THROUGH THE FIRE WITH YOU

(S. Quatro/S.Roden/L.Tuckey/A. Scott/S.Grant)

Butterfly/Rak, Singing Earth music Ltd. Fanfare pub.

CHORUS
I'LL WALK THROUGH THE FIRE WITH YOU
I'LL DREAM EVERY DREAM WITH YOU
I'LL LOOK IN YOUR EYES, I'LL TELL YOU NO LIES
I'LL WALK THROUGH THE FIRE WITH YOU

V1
IT'S BEING TOO CLOSE THAT KEEPS US SO FAR APART
WE GET BURNED BY EACH OTHER'S LIGHT
BUT WE SHARE THE SAME HEART
TOO MANY WORDS, TOO MANY FIGHTS
TOO MANY FEARS, AND SLEEPLESS NIGHTS

REPEAT CHORUS

V2
THE TRUTH IS TOO HARD,
BUT YOU DON'T LIKE THE GAME WHEN I PLAY IT
THE TRUTH IS, YOU HEAR WHAT YOU WANT TO HEAR,
AND I HAD TO HURT YOU TO SAY IT
ARE WE SO DIFFERENT, ARE WE THE SAME
WHEN PUSH COMES TO SHOVE, WE'RE BOTH TO BLAME

REPEAT CHORUS

BRIDGE
IT TOOK SO LONG TO UNDERSTAND
AND ALL YOU HAD TO DO WAS, TAKE MY HAND
AND EVERYTHING WE SAY, MAKES ME WALK AWAY
I DON'T WANT TO HEAR IT NOW
BUT IT'S GOTTA BE SAID, AND HOW
LET'S WALK THROUGH THE FIRE

REPEAT CHORUS

Featured on Back to the Drive 2006

And for the final entry in the book. This nearly didn't make it because to be quite honest, I had overlooked it. My songwriting partner on this pointed it out to me, sent me the lyrics and I went wow... so... here it is. Seems a fitting way to end the book.

We had been on my Russian tour in 1989, the beginning of Glasnost, and it left an indelible mark on us all. This came after a discussion about Lenin's tomb and his body lying there, and how strange the whole thing was/is.

• 2019, waiting to go on, from the shadows to the spotlight.

BETWEEN LIFE AND DEATH

(S. Quatro / R. Wolfe) Butterfly/Rak Pub.

V1
BETWEEN LIFE AND DEATH
LIES VELVET UNDER STEEL
BEHIND GLASS THAT CANNOT HIDE
AND THE FEAR WE FEEL
THIN DIVIDING LINE SO REAL
BETWEEN LIFE AND DEATH
WHERE WE LEARN TO FORGET AH AH AH

V2
A CRIPPLED HAND THAT COULD NOT SHAKE
ONE OPEN HAND WOULDN'T WAKE
TWO SIGHTLESS EYES WE COULD NOT SEE
YOU TRAPPED A NATION TO SET IT FREE
TO SET IT FREE

V3
NO BONES TO ASHES, NO DUST TO FALL
ONE UNMARKED GRAVE IN A GRANITE WALL
PROCESSIONS PASSING TWO BY TWO
CURIOSITIES DANCE OF DEATH TO VIEW

CHORUS
BETWEEN LIFE AND DEATH
WHERE WE LEARN TO FORGET
NO SIGHT (BETWEEN LIFE AND)
NO BREATH (BETWEEN LIFE AND)
HE'S GOT NO RIGHT (NO SIGHT NO)
NO WRONG (BETWEEN LIFE AND BREATH)

V4
QUIET STILL SO MANY YEARS
WHEN FREEDOM TALKS NO ONE HEARS
WHEN FAITH CAN BREAK THIS FAITHLESS WALL
IT'S MY BELIEF THAT IT WILL, THAT IT WILL FALL
REPEAT CHORUS
BETWEEN LIFE AND DEATH
WHERE WE LEARN TO FORGET

Never released, demo only

www.ingramcontent.com/pod-product-compliance
Lightning Source LLC
Chambersburg PA
CBHW061232150426

42812CB00054BA/2571